101 WAYS TO
BETTER
PRESENTATIONS

ELIZABETH TIERNEY

**KOGAN
PAGE**

First published in 1999

Kogan Page Limited
120 Pentonville Road
London N1 9JN
UK

Kogan Page Limited
163 Central Avenue, Suite 4
Dover, NH 03820
USA

British Library Cataloguing in Publication Data

A CIP record for this book is available from the British Library.

ISBN 0 7494 2968 2

Typeset by Jean Cussons Typesetting, Diss, Norfolk
Printed and bound by Clays Ltd, St Ives plc

Contents

CONTENTS

CONTENTS

CONTENTS

Introduction

If we were asked to name our greatest fear in doing business, many of us would admit that we are terrified at the notion of having to speak before a group. For good reason: it's a daunting experience. But it is an essential part of doing business. Think about it. We have to give talks of one kind or another frequently. In one week, busy business-people may be called upon to speak to the Board of Directors on Monday, to 10 colleagues at a departmental meeting on Tuesday morning, to 50 interested investors on Wednesday, to their personal staff of three in the office on Thursday, to a hiring panel on Friday or to an audience of 300 at a conference held at a hotel on Saturday. That's six presentations. Your list is probably longer. But it may have to be if you wish to be successful.

Because speaking in public is as unnerving an experience as it is, this book is written to help you decrease some of the anxiety that you are feeling as well as to offer recommendations for enhancing your talks. To do that, the book examines the process from beginning to end and offers you *101 Ways to Better Presentations*.

While making a presentation is a complete event in and of itself, this book breaks the whole into parts. This enables you to better understand the process you are involved in when you give a talk. The better you understand the process, the more confident, credible and effective you will be as a speaker.

Let's be frank. One of the reasons that we are all as concerned as we are about speaking is that we simply don't want to make fools of ourselves in front of other people. We don't want to say or do something that appears stupid or thoughtless to the others present. But even knowing that such a possibility might happen, speaking in public can not and should not be avoided. You have an opportunity to influence others, to demonstrate your talents and to represent your organization.

You may say or hope that current computer technology will allow more of us to work in the privacy of our own offices or homes rather than in the workplace. Even so, there will be many times when you will be asked to defend or explain your ideas or your work in progress to others in an open forum rather than in a 'chat room'. In fact, with video phones and teleconferencing becoming more of a reality, we will be more visible than ever.

One
Good Speakers

Let's begin. Think about effective speakers you have heard throughout your life and in your career. Who are they? As you think of them, you may notice that they have come from all walks of life. You have probably identified politicians, members of the clergy, educators, athletes, entertainers or business people. Can you identify why you recall them? What particular characteristic brought them to mind? Whatever the specific reason you remember them, they reached you.

Quite simply, good speakers have an impact on others. They are memorable. One reason that you haven't forgotten them is that they recognize they have the ability to make a difference in their audience's lives. And they use it. Good speakers also respect their audiences and understand the communication process. Effective speakers also know what ensures successful communication and what prevents it. They know their own weaknesses as speakers and try to eliminate them. They use their strengths.

WAY 1   BE AWARE OF YOUR IMPACT ON OTHERS

First of all, as we said, good speakers recognize that they can make a difference to their listeners. They appreciate that the talk they are giving can affect the people to whom they are speaking. They recognize that they can make the audience laugh, take notice or cry. They can also make an audience angry.

The topic may not always be monumental. Speakers may be suggesting ideas that may make your life easier or make it more difficult. They may be recommending dress-down

3

days on Fridays, the take-over of another company, or the purchase of a particular service or product. The topic may not be of great consequence. While you may not consider introducing dress-down days as earth-shattering, they may be a morale booster for the audience. Therefore, suggesting the idea may indicate to the listeners that the speaker is sensitive to their situations and to their needs in the work environment.

Effective speakers recognize the opportunities they have for making change, and they seize the moment. They do not assume that the only important talks that they are going to make are at annual presentations to the Board of Directors or at the Eastern Regional Sales Conference. They know that short in-company talks in their own offices count, too. For you to be good as a speaker, you have to believe that your ideas are important. So, it doesn't matter if you are speaking to a group of five in your office or to a group of 400 in Brussels and New York in a video-conference.

Unlike dress-down days, introducing the notion of a take-over may have powerful financial implications for individuals and organizations. While there may be great risks, the potential exists for great opportunities. In the same way, if you can convince someone to buy your product, that purchase may enhance the way they live or work. Your widget may save money, time or human resources for them and increase your profits, too. In effect, when you speak never underestimate the significance of your words to the people listening to you.

WAY 2   UNDERSTAND THE COMMUNICATION PROCESS

Successful athletes, musicians, politicians and business people know their trades. In the same way, effective speakers should understand what they are actually doing when they communicate. Even though it may seem artificial to examine what we take for granted and do every day, it is helpful to consider the individual components in the communication process. While much of the process is instantaneous, by breaking it down into a series of steps, you are better able to analyse what you do well or what needs to be improved. In fact, after thinking about the process, you may discover that you will have second thoughts about being a spontaneous presenter. Many speakers believe that they don't need to plan or practise, that they can 'shoot from the hip' and still be successful.

Before we look at each step in more depth, let's examine what we do when we communicate:

- We have a thought or an idea which we will call a message.
- We want to share that notion or message with an audience.
- We determine the best way to express that message.
- We share the message.
- We anticipate feedback.
- We react to the feedback.

Suppose your idea is to institute dress-down days on Fridays. You have heard from some colleagues in other organizations that people are more energized at the prospect of wearing less formal clothes once a week. Human resource departments have noticed that absenteeism is lower on Fridays than it had been and that people are less stressed and more motivated the rest of the week. Let's analyse the communication that occurs.

Step one: you believe you have a good idea for your company or your division. At this point it is an idea. It is in your head. But the notion of 'dress-down Fridays' isn't going to be considered at all much less put into practice unless you share it with others.

Step two: you want to share your idea about dress-down days with the other decision-makers.

Step three: you decide the best way to communicate the idea. You consider phoning. Then you decide that a face-to-face meeting is better. You weigh dropping by some strategic offices to chat. But you dismiss both plans and decide to include the recommendation for dress-down days in your presentation at the next department meeting.

Step four: you share the idea. You present your recommendation at 2.30 on Monday in the conference room.

Step five: you anticipate feedback. You know that some people will reject the notion out of hand and that others may consider it seriously. Some people may actually laugh at you. Someone may thank you for suggesting the idea. You may be challenged to justify your thinking. All of these are reactions to your remarks. They represent feedback

Step six: you react to that feedback. You take what you were told and learnt at the meeting. You combine this with your own views of dress-down days. You then modify the idea. Based on the feedback, you may decide to overcome some of the specific objections, to restate your case or perhaps to drop the idea altogether. Unless you drop the idea altogether, you will be starting the communication process again by having a revised idea and the cycle begins once more.

WAY 3 KNOW WHAT PREVENTS COMMUNICATION

By considering communication as a series of steps, you can determine where breakdowns may occur. Good speakers recognize that even the most effective communication can be blocked. That blockage may occur for many reasons. To eliminate problems you try to control as much of the process as you can. But once you send your message, it is out of your hands. Your ideas are in the hands and minds of your receivers. But until then it is yours to weigh and consider.

Let's look at some of the problems that may occur.

Suppose you have an idea that is unclear. It may be unclear because you have not been able to make yourself understood. This often happens when ideas have not been thought through sufficiently or what you want to share may be too abstract.

Now suppose you decide to share your idea with someone else. But if you haven't analysed your audience well enough, you risk being misunderstood or not understood at all. We will talk more about audience in Way 6. If you haven't anticipated your audience's reactions, your message won't be received. Beware of making generalizations or assumptions about audiences:

- Don't make assumptions about the audience's level of knowledge.
- Don't speak over their heads.
- Don't alienate them by speaking down to them either.

Audiences are all different because they consist of diverse individuals in different roles with differing experiences. Thus, they may have differing reactions to what you are saying.

Now suppose you have selected a way to transmit your message. But if you haven't selected the *best* way to send that message, your ideas may not be received. Why?

- If you pick the wrong approach, you decrease the chances of your audience understanding what you are saying.
- If you whisper, you may not be heard.
- If you include too many visuals, your images may overwhelm the audience.
- If you use the wrong words, you may be misinterpreted.
- If you don't compensate for extraneous noises, you will not be heard.
- If you don't consider the impact of the time or the place, you may have an audience that is distracted.

Good speakers recognize that it is easy for a message to be lost or misconstrued. Therefore, they carefully consider their options and make thoughtful choices before they communicate. Consequently they will not regret what they did after they have spoken.

WAY 4   IDENTIFY AND ELIMINATE YOUR WEAKNESSES

You have seen the steps that are involved in the communication process. You can recognize where and how blockages may occur. For you to become a more effective speaker you should examine your own communication style to determine where or how it may be breaking down. You may logically ask, 'How do I become more aware of my own presentation style?'

- You can take courses in public speaking or in presentation.
- You can read books; try *101 Ways to Better Communication* from this series, for instance.
- You can ask a colleague for feedback on a presentation.
- You can record yourself on a camcorder and view the video.
- You can record yourself on an audiotape and listen to the recording.
- You can do all of the above.

'But what should I look for?' you ask. The answer to that question will become clearer as you read through the rest of the Ways. Look for physical aspects of your presentation that may be problematic to an audience. Consider how you appear. Listen to how you sound. Analyse the organization of your talk. Then think about your talk in terms of your specific audience.

'What if I discover a problem?' you ask. Suppose you identify an aspect of your presentation style that might prevent effective communication. Work at eliminating it. Be realistic. The change won't happen overnight. It takes time. You eliminate any habit, strategy or technique by catching yourself in the act and trying to change it. But it takes a number of repetitions before it is ingrained.

Suppose you are told about a problem or you spot it yourself when you play back a cassette tape. You learn that you lose the audience because you speak too quickly when you give presentations. To remedy the problem, make a deliberate effort to speak more slowly.

Suppose after watching a videotape of yourself, you realize that you confuse the audience because you try to include too much material and your talks aren't structured well enough. To remedy the problem, work at organizing your thoughts better.

Of course, there are times that you will be required to speak spontaneously, but more often than not, you will have time to prepare. Don't berate yourself or become overzealous in your determination to reach your goal of excellence as a speaker. Select one area of weakness at a time and work at correcting it. Once you are comfortable with the adjustment, then identify another element that you want to modify and change that one. Good speakers evolve over time with hard work.

WAY 5   IDENTIFY AND BUILD ON YOUR STRENGTHS

Most of us find it easy to criticize ourselves and to identify what we do wrong. In fact, most of us believe that we have many weaknesses. Most of us assume that we are awful speakers, which is why we are so frightened by the prospect of making presentations. Well, the truth is that you are probably doing any number of things well. Yes, good speakers work at eliminating their weaknesses. But good speakers recognize their strengths and build on them. Consider some of these attributes:

- You have a good clear speech pattern.
- You find it easy to present ideas in a simple form.
- You have a sense of humour.
- You have an easy-going manner.
- You have a beautiful voice.

One or all of them are pluses. Each one can enhance your presentation. When you listen to yourself on a tape, when you see yourself played back on a video, or when you ask for a colleague's opinion, be sure to determine exactly what you did that is good. Focus on the positives, not just on the negatives. What you want to do when you are developing as a speaker is to use your strengths at the same time as you are progressively and systematically eliminating the weakness or weaknesses that detract from your work.

Two
Your Audience

We said earlier that an essential part of the communication process is having an idea or thought that you want to share. The notion of sharing is essential to the process. If you write a letter that you never put in the post, you aren't sharing your ideas. If you whisper a talk so that no one in the room can hear you, you aren't sharing. To be effective as a speaker, you should spend time thinking about the people with whom you are sharing your ideas. You need to consider your audience.

WAY 6   GET AN OVERVIEW

When you are asked to give a talk or to make a report to a group, it is vital that you get a general impression of the people to whom you will be speaking. Often a supervisor may say, 'I want you to speak at the annual meeting in February and at the April board meeting.' You may be invited to speak at a management seminar or at a breakfast meeting about marketing strategies. You may be asked to speak about computer applications at a conference.

Too often, however, when we are asked to speak, we focus on the invitation and on the person who extended it. We are flattered, excited or delighted. Our egos are fed by the recognition. We are thrilled and then terrified at the prospect. If this reaction is true for you, rein in your conflicting emotions. Then remember to ask questions about your audience to get an overview of who will be present. Ask why the meeting is being held. Find out how many people will attend and ask about their general areas of expertise. Replace your emotional reaction with some invaluable hard data.

WAY 7   INVESTIGATE THE SPECIFICS

While an overview is important, don't stop there. You need details. Suppose you have been asked to speak to the board or to a group at a conference. You have determined how many will be present. You also know the purpose of the meeting. But you have other questions to ask. While they may not suit every situation, some of them might include:

- What are their job titles?
- What is their native language? Does every one speak English?
- Where are they from? What country? What region?
- What are their ages?
- How many men? How many women?
- What do they know about the subject?
- What is their training?
- Why are they attending?
- Who else will be speaking?
- If there are other speakers, what are their subjects?

It takes only a few minutes to ask the organizer questions like these. But ask them. The more you know about the audience the more you can tailor what you are going to say to them. Thus you are ensuring that you will be understood. And you will not have mis-communication. The answers to your questions may help you decide about the amount of explaining you will have to do, the types of visuals you should use, or the approach that you might take. For example, analogies to American football may not work well with a group of French men and women. References to crowded buses, trains and airports may not be appropriate for a talk in a rural area. Nor will the agonies of snow shovelling be readily understood in mild climates. In the same way a group of marketing managers may require more background on the financials of a recommendation than those trained in accountancy. Get details.

WAY 8   DON'T UNDERESTIMATE ANYONE

When you are asking your questions about the audience,

try to get as many names and job titles as you can. The more you know about what people actually do, the better you can adapt your subject to their expertise.

However, once you know who is attending, be careful. Many speakers make unwise assumptions. They learn that the MD, CEO or divisional manager will be in attendance. Because they consider the position important to the decision-making process, such speakers decide to pitch the entire talk to that person. That is not a sensible decision for two reasons. First, you can alienate other people in the room if you are discounting them and directing your thoughts to the head person. Second, you are making assumptions about who has influence over whom or whose opinions are sought out or valued by that senior manager. Frequently, senior people ask the opinions of their assistants. Remember even Don Corleone had a *consigliere*. You may not know who that person or people may be. Therefore, address everyone present even if it is a mixture of management and support staff. Value everyone present. Prepare your thoughts with the entire audience in mind.

WAY 9 ASSESS THEIR MOTIVATION

Based on who is going to be present, determine what they know about your subject. Also think about or try to discover, if you can, why they will be attending. In many instances the audience's level of interest will affect their reactions to what you are saying. For example:

- Find out if people want to be there or have been ordered to be.
- Find out if people were sent to the meeting because someone else didn't want to attend.
- Find out if someone thought that attending would be important for a specific person's development or position.

If you are speaking at a conference, consider how many people are attending the meeting because it is an opportunity to spend a weekend in Paris or because they genuinely value the issues being addressed by those who are speaking. In essence, the motivation of the people in front of you affects your planning of your presentation.

WAY 10   CONSIDER THE POLITICS

People have influence over each other. Organizations are political. Neither overestimate nor underestimate that fact when you are talking to a group. While some people take only their own counsel, most of us weigh the opinions of others before making final decisions.

Don't forget that some members of your audience may have their own personal political agendas. They may want to demonstrate their intellect or their ability to confront or argue, not so much to challenge your ideas but to demonstrate their skills in front of the others in the room. In other words, questions from some people may derive more from their own needs than from the issues that you are raising in your presentation.

Don't forget, too, that some people may be resentful of others because they were ordered to attend the meeting. Other people may be feeling proud because they were told that they would benefit.

Therefore, when you consider the actual individuals in your audience and their positions, also consider their relationships to and with each other:

- Are people genuinely interested in your subject?
- Are people present who are seeking to advance their careers?
- Have some others been denied recent promotions?
- Are some people waiting for contract agreements to be settled?
- Are some people feeling that they know more than others because they have worked for the company longer and yet can not advance because they lack the appropriate credentials?
- Are some people jealous of your opportunity to speak?

Having some sense of the political dynamics is useful, but don't over-analyse. When members of the audience ask you questions, you should think about where those questions are coming from. Think about what is motivating your questioners and who they may be trying to impress. Consider the implication of different jobs and titles on attitudes toward your topic. Consider differing perspectives. The more you take the make up of your audience into your planning, the more effective your talk will be.

Three
Your Content

You can analyse your audience, respect their abilities and diversity and admire their talent. You can not totally control them. However, you can control the content of the talk you are giving. So, let's take a hard look at the message you intend to share.

WAY 11   HAVE A MESSAGE

Advising you to 'have a message' may sound pretty basic. When we were children we may have been told, 'Don't say anything unless you have something to say.' What does it mean? It means that you should have ideas that are important enough to share. When you think about the talks that you have heard throughout your life, you will remember some good and some poor ones. Perhaps one of the basic problems with the poor talks was that the speech suffered because the message was not clear to the speaker. Under those circumstances, the ideas become vague or waffly to the audience.

To be a good speaker you need to know 'exactly' what you want to talk about, not just 'sort of' know. Let's suppose that you plan to evaluate levels of productivity, or to give a monthly departmental progress report or to discuss an adjustment in the budget. You know you have to say something about productivity, progress or the budget. 'Yes', you say, 'I have something to say about productivity, progress or the budget.' Yes, that's a good start for your planning but it is not enough of a message for a talk. You have to know exactly what that 'something' is.

WAY 12   KNOW YOUR PURPOSE

You may say, 'Of course, I know my purpose. Didn't I just mention that we were going to talk about productivity, progress or the budget?' Yes, but let's step back for a moment. Let's take those dress-down days we mentioned earlier. Suppose that's your message, but you have to do some more thinking. To be effective you should be able to articulate precisely why you are talking about dress-down days.

In the same way you need to be able to say *why* you are talking about productivity and how you intend to influence the audience's thinking about the subject. What is it about the budget that is important for this audience to understand? Are you overspending? Is there a surplus in some area? Do you need to anticipate a major expenditure? Having a purpose means knowing what you want the audience to do or say or think as a result of what you are telling them. It isn't enough to say, 'I'm talking about dress-down days'. You have to be able to articulate first to yourself and then to the audience why what you are saying matters. You want your listeners to consider your subject for a reason. If you can not articulate why the audience will benefit from hearing your progress report, you will be less successful as a speaker. Audiences are more attentive when they believe that the subject is relevant to them.

A good speaker doesn't expect the audience to make the right assumptions. A good speaker assumes the responsibility of both knowing the message and explaining its purpose.

WAY 13   ANTICIPATE OBJECTIONS

In order to anticipate objections you have to take into account your knowledge of the audience. You can not anticipate challenges if you haven't thought about who will be listening to you. The more you know about the make up of your group the better able you are to put yourself into their shoes. Only then can you try to think from their unique perspectives.

Your knowledge of the audience's personalities, responsibilities and attitudes helps you determine which elements of your talk might be challenged or which of your ideas might be dismissed as being lightweight or frivolous. Suppose your talk focuses on the importance of using the Internet. The company has spent vast sums on upgrading computers, but you know that many people are still using them as somewhere to put their Post-its or as knick-knack shelves. You need to be sensitive to their level of knowledge and awareness. Otherwise, your talk will fall on deaf ears.

A talk to members of a creative department might be different from a talk to a group of financial planners. A talk on the same subject to management might be different from one given to a group in editorial. When you prepare your talk, you should think about what arguments might arise based on the perspectives of your audience. Build your responses right into the talk. If you can anticipate the creative department's concerns, then you can indicate to them your awareness by saying, 'Some of you may not agree that the use of the Internet will allow you to… but it can, because…'. When you don't anticipate certain fundamental arguments, you may find that your audience is resisting your ideas from the outset. You can free them to listen by overcoming their objections.

WAY 14   ELIMINATE THE NON-ESSENTIAL

Often talks are too general. Frequently they are loaded with unnecessary verbiage. Remember that your objective is to get your message across to your audience. Your message is what you want people to do or to understand as a result of what you say. Therefore, if you clutter your talk with tangential data, interesting anecdotes about trips you have taken or endless implementation strategies, more than likely very little of your message will be understood, recalled or acted upon.

In essence the phrase, 'Keep it simple, stupid' is as true for speeches as it is for much else. As you review your talk be sure that everything that you are including relates directly to what you are trying to convince the audience to do. Even if your talk is intended to introduce another speaker at a meeting or to provide an entertaining chat at a dinner, stay on your topic. Don't wander. If you are asked to praise Caesar, don't spend five minutes discussing how nervous you are about speaking – unless of course, Caesar has been helping you to overcome your nervousness. True, you may be attached to some of your stories, analogies or data. Remember good stories won't go bad. You can always use your data or your anecdotes in other speeches where they are more appropriate.

WAY 15   CHOOSE AN APPROACH

At this point, you know what you are going to say, and you know why you are going to say it. You have also thought about the nature of your audience. Therefore, you realize where in the talk you might have to clarify or support your ideas because of their differing viewpoints. You have accomplished a great deal.

There is more to do. Now you have to choose your approach. A formal 20-minute talk may not be appropriate for a breakfast meeting or a lunch at a nearby pub. You have to think about the situation and the setting. So instead of talking all the time, you may decide to talk for five minutes and answer questions for 15. A 20-minute talk on a complex subject may require you to use more visuals than for one that is less complicated. Given the subject or the time, you may want to keep the talk light-hearted and casual, or you may want it to be earnest and serious.

- Perhaps you want to talk at the audience the whole time.
- Perhaps you want to involve them not only by having them ask questions, but also by having them do something.
- Perhaps you want a roundtable discussion after you have spoken.
- Perhaps you want to raise questions and allow people to talk to their neighbours before answering you.

In other words, depending upon the situation, the topic, your purpose and your audience, you should select an approach that will best accomplish your goal, which remains the same – getting your message across.

Four
The Beginning

Talks have a beginning, a middle and an end. Because the beginning and the end are typically the parts that people remember well, you should spend some time determining how best to begin and end. Don't forget that when you present information orally, you are asking people to retain that information by using primarily only one of their senses: listening.

Your listeners lead busy lives. They have families, cars, bills, jobs, homes, groceries. Even returning videos to the shop takes time. Your job as a speaker is to get people to pay attention to you from the moment you begin. You have to organize your thoughts to ensure that their minds don't wander back to their own concerns. If your audience is distracted by internal or external interference, they won't listen. They will hear their inner thoughts, and they won't hear your words. Thus, they won't act on your message.

WAY 16   MAKE A GOOD FIRST IMPRESSION

Most of us make judgements about other people within seconds of seeing or meeting them. Right or wrong, as members of the audience we look at speakers before their talks and make decisions about them. We look at the height, shape, age, sex, or colour of the person who is going to speak and make a judgement. We look at the way speakers move or dress and we evaluate them. All of this happens before the speakers have even said a word.

With that reality in mind, it is important for you to put your best foot forward before you begin. So, when you do begin to speak, your opening words need to be well-chosen. The beginning of your talk isn't the time for you to be adjusting your clothing, fiddling with papers, or apologizing for being late. This isn't the time to straighten a tie or tap on the mike. What you do first is what the audience remembers. Therefore, the beginning is the time to look at the audience, smile and then utter your well-prepared opening sentence.

WAY 17   USE MOTIVATIONAL TECHNIQUES

As we said, the beginning of your talk is when you want to grab the audience's attention. There are a number of tried and tested techniques you may want to consider using:

- Open with a quotation.
- Ask a question.
- Tell a story or anecdote.
- Make a provocative statement.
- Use a shocking statistic.
- Show a well-designed visual.

In other words, assume that the audience is still focused on what they were doing just before they sat down or came into the room. That's where their minds are. They are preoccupied with what they just heard, with conversations they were having, with their personal lives, with the lunches they didn't care for, coffee they meant to get, or a report they have to finish.

You, as speaker, have the job of distracting them from their own thoughts and giving them a reason to be more interested in your ideas than in their current ones. Your well-chosen opening words and actions can do just that.

WAY 18   STATE YOUR PURPOSE

While it is important that your opening words have the effect of getting your audience's attention and taking them away from their own concerns or pressures, you can not stop there:

- You now have to hold their attention by clearly stating your purpose.
- You have to tell them why your subject matter has an impact on them.
- You need to give them a reason for needing your information.
- You need to connect your subject matter to their jobs or responsibilities.

In essence, you have to make your ideas relevant. How often have you heard talks and weren't exactly sure what the speaker was going on about and what it had to do with you? Speakers frequently do not make an explicit statement about the purpose of the talk. You should.

Once you have made your strong opening sentence, told a story or a joke, you should explain how that story or joke relates to the message. Don't be afraid to state your purpose. Do not assume that your listeners know your intent just because they received a memo inviting them to the meeting or a programme with the title of your talk printed on it.

Consider saying something like, 'We are here to discuss the implications of budget cuts on the company restaurant,' or 'This morning we will examine the proposed changes in the accounting system and its impact on your department.' However you choose to say it, that kind of statement clarifies your purpose for your audience. They know what you plan to do, or at least part of it.

WAY 19   EXPLAIN YOUR APPROACH

You have given the audience a reason to listen. You have their attention. You have told them what you are going to discuss. Now tell them what approach you are going to use to explain your view or to support your position. You are giving them a road map and telling them how you are going to get them there and how long it is going to take. You might say, 'In the next 20 minutes we will discuss four aspects of our investigation into our current appraisal system. First, we will examine the problems we have experienced with the appraisal system. Second, we will explain how we analysed those problems. Third, we will present our conclusions, and fourth, we will make two recommendations to simplify the process and to eliminate the problems we have identified to ensure that the appraisal system is a more effective one.'

Tell the audience exactly what you are going to do. Never forget, as we said before, that for the most part you are asking people to retain information by depending on their ability to listen. The road map that you give them will help them anticipate where you are going and how long it will take. Remember what you asked your parents or what your little ones ask you: 'Are we there yet?' To avoid that question, as a speaker, tell your audience where you are going, how long it will take and how you are going to get there.

Five
The Middle

The beginning of your talk is when you get the audience's attention, present you message and explain your purpose and approach. The middle section provides you with the opportunity to present your ideas in an orderly fashion. To help your listeners stay focused and retain information provide them with a structure.

WAY 20   STRUCTURE YOUR THOUGHTS

When you are putting your thoughts together or looking through your material in preparation for your talk, try to find a natural structure. Ask yourself:

- Can you break down your topic into two parts such as causes and effects or advantages and disadvantages?
- Can you organize your material from an historical perspective? Can you plan to discuss what used to be, what currently is and what will be?
- Can you use a SWOT analysis? Can you discuss strengths, weaknesses, opportunities and threats?
- Can you present your research by asking a question, showing the methodology for answering the question, explaining the findings and making the recommendations?

There is no one way or perfect model to use every time you speak. The nature of your topic should determine the structure.

It is helpful to you and to your audience if you select a clear structure. 'How do you identify one?' you ask. The process is no different from the one you use if you were writing a report. In a report you look for some natural order that will enable your readers to follow your logic. The same is true for listeners. Remember though, with a report, readers can always return to a previous paragraph or section if they get lost. Listeners can not. If you don't have a structure and the audience gets lost, they may not be able to find you again. They may not want to find you.

WAY 21   USE NUMBERS

You have decided on a basic structure for your talk, such as cause and effect, before and after, advantages or disadvantages, or conclusions and recommendations. Think now about how you can create another internal order within one or more of those sections.

One way to organize is to use numbers. 'This morning we are going to examine five methods for insuring that we eliminate our problems with the new phone system.' Begin by saying 'First', and discuss point one. Follow this by saying 'Second' and then discuss point two and so on. When you tell your audience to expect five items, they will expect five. Don't discuss four points or seven points instead of what you promised.

I remember one speaker who said, 'I am going to show you 18 changes that are going to affect the tourist industry in the future.' He then systematically discussed number one through to 18. I looked around the room when he began. Like the others around me, I immediately numbered one to 18 on the back of a handout. We were ready to pay attention. He discussed 18 items, not 12 and not 19.

If you do decide to use numbers, be sure to say the number before you make the next point. 'The third reason we are working during the holiday... .' When you announce how many items to expect repeat each number before you start that section. People will better remember your reasoning.

WAY 22   CONSIDER CHRONOLOGY

Another method of helping your audience retain information is to structure your thoughts chronologically. What you do is discuss what happened in the past, continue into the present and then forecast the future. You can use reverse chronology if you wish. Either way you have created an order.

If you are describing an event such as an accident that occurred in a short period of time, you can do the same thing: what happened first, then 10 minutes later, then 15 minutes after that. Only you can make the decision about whether chronology works for you. The nature of your subject may dictate it. Remember, too, depending on the age or knowledge of your audience, if you use chronology you may need to provide an historical context. You may begin by indicating that 'Not all of you were here three years ago when we instituted the flex-time scheduling. Therefore, let's first look at what we were experiencing when we introduced it.'

WAY 23   WEIGH THE IMPORTANCE

When you structure your thoughts, you may decide that some of your ideas or recommendations are weightier than others. You believe that the audience will value some of your ideas more than others. Thus, you may want to put your recommendations in the order of their importance. Remember most of us retain first and last items in a series better than the items in the middle.

Thus, you may want to put your most vital point first and then your others in a descending order of importance. You may want to reverse it. Have an important point first, a relatively weak one in the middle and the strongest as the last one. You are deciding that you want the audience to remember what you said just before you walked away from them.

Again, it doesn't matter which order you select. But, you should have an order. Bear in mind, whichever order you pick – strongest argument first or last – you should be consistent whenever you repeat the same items. Stay in the same order in the beginning, in the middle and in the end of your talk.

WAY 24   REPEAT, REPEAT, REPEAT

Speaking of repetition, let's emphasize the importance of repeating. People are depending primarily on their ears for absorbing what you are saying. Repeat. Repeat. Repeat and repeat. If you make a point about accountability in the opening, there is nothing to prevent you from saying it again in the middle of the talk. And you should be sure to say it again in the last section.

Suppose your position is that flex-time will make a difference for morale or for saving expenses. Say it several times. What you want is for people to leave your meeting with those words in their heads. Advertisers do it. Politicians do it. Repeat the words or sentences that you want people to remember. We are not talking about creating a mantra. But repeat your key ideas enough for the points to be brought home.

Repetition is important if you are using numbers, too. 'We have considered the first reason, cost. Now let's look at the second, quality.' Then in the conclusion you speak of the two reasons, cost and quality.

WAY 25   USE MNEMONICS

Another way of aiding memory is by using mnemonics. These are devices designed to help us recall. Some of us create them in our everyday lives. Perhaps your computer password, your voice-mail code or your pin number for the automatic teller machine at the bank are mnemonics.

Suppose your mnemonic is the list of chores that you have to do when you leave the office. For example, you use the word DEAL to remind you to pick up the Dog from the vet, buy some Eggs in the shop, get cash at the ATM and collect the Lawnmower from the repair shop. Sounds silly, but we all create ways of keeping information in our heads. Given how hectic life is these days, we need other methods besides writing in our filofaxes or personal organizers. Sometimes just a word or phrase will do.

The same technique for aiding memory is useful for some talks. If you see that you can create a memorable word or phrase from the first letter of the key words or ideas in your arguments, then do so. The audience may remember. But be sure that they remember what the letters represent and don't walk away only remembering your mnemonic.

WAY 26   CLARIFY SPATIAL RELATIONS

Much of what we talk about nowadays in a global economy involves location or geography. If you are talking about your global network, your new office lay-out, your new offices or even your new logo, it is helpful to make a conscious effort to work from top to bottom, from bottom to top, from left to right or from right to left.

If you are describing the plan for your new offices, take the audience from the entrance to the rear, or move them around the offices in a clockwise or counter-clockwise direction. It is easier to visualize or retain. If you are talking about doing business in different countries, try to move around the globe in a specific direction – east to west, west to east, north to south and so on.

Six
The End

The beginning of a talk is the opportunity to get your audience's attention. The middle is the section that permits you to develop your ideas. The final part allows you to recapitulate your ideas or present conclusions or recommendations in as clear and strong a way as possible. Your audience is left with your ideas clearly in their minds, and you put them there.

WAY 27 RESTATE YOUR POINT NOT YOUR CLOSING

We have already indicated several times that repetition is essential when you are relying primarily on an audience's ears. Unless you sell recordings or give them a transcript at the door, your talk will have been all they have of your ideas. And they will have heard it only once. Therefore, don't be bashful about saying again at the end what you said at the outset or what has appeared as a theme throughout. 'Therefore, in conclusion, we recommend that…' Say it again.

Now this may sound silly, but when you say that you are concluding, please conclude. The number of speakers who say that they are about to conclude and then continue for another five minutes is amazing. Some speakers say, 'In conclusion', followed shortly thereafter by 'Finally', and then 'One last point before I leave you.' Once you signal that you are concluding by using words that indicate an ending, end.

WAY 28 WRAP THE PACKAGE

Your entire talk is a package. It should sound as if it has

been put together, wrapped and tied up neatly. You do that in part by having the end mirror the beginning. When you decide how you are going to structure your talk and how you are going to begin it, be sure that your ending is consistent with that opening.

- If you decided to begin with a joke, conclude with a similar related joke.
- If you began with a quotation, there is no harm in ending with a similarly appropriate quotation.
- If you begin with a mnemonic, repeat it at the end.
- If you began with a question, ask another one or repeat your original question and answer it.
- If you begin with a frightening statistic, end with another sort of statistic.

In other words, look at the way you have organized your talk and make sure that the ending is consistent with and reinforces what you have said in your opening remarks. 'That is why I began by saying…'

WAY 29   DON'T FADE AWAY

Remember your closing remarks are critical for your listeners. End with a strong statement and with a strong image. Avoid having your last words be some sort of apologetic closing like, 'I hope I haven't take up too much of your time', or 'I am sorry that we ran a few minutes late', or 'Thank you for listening.' Such comments may seem charming, self-effacing or polite, but what these words do is distract from your final, powerful words about your message. What the audience hears last is your apology when what they should be hearing is your view of the issues.

Make your final statement. Take a deep breath. Wait. Look around. If you feel you should do so, say one brief 'Thank you'. It is enough. Then, unless you are taking questions from the floor, take your seat. Don't drop your shoulders, mop your brow, throw your eyes to the heavens or let out a sigh of relief. Maintain a strong, memorable positive image.

Seven
Your Word Choices

Having a worthwhile idea is essential to giving a powerful talk. But you see it takes more than a good idea to create an excellent speech. Structuring your talk is important too. So is selecting your words well. The concept, the structure and the words are all essential parts of an effective talk. Avoiding jargon, explaining technical language and watching for colloquialisms and idiosyncrasies are ways of enhancing a talk.

WAY 30   AVOID JARGON

Time and again you have heard the phrase 'Avoid jargon'. But it is easy to fall into using it, especially if you work with people who write or speak it in the office. It's remarkable how words like 'transparent' or 'synergistic' become commonplace in a short time. Some people seem to think that it is mundane to 'talk' or 'meet'. Apparently 'inter-facing' or 'liaising' with a member of a committee is an executive privilege while talking is not. 'Meet' and 'talk' are perfectly good words and are readily understood by most of us, so use them.

However, if your intention is to confuse your listeners, then by all means use jargon. Certainly have a 'conflagra-tion' rather than a 'fire'. Speak of inputs, outputs and throughputs. But if you want to keep your message clear and easily understood, keep it simple and avoid jargon.

WAY 31   EXPLAIN TECHNICAL LANGUAGE

Another tendency many of us have is to use the technical language of our specializations as if the vocabulary were common to everyone. Doctors do it. Lawyers do it.

Computer analysts do it. Marketing executives do it. Hoteliers do it. Every field has its own unique vocabulary. But be sure that your particular audience is familiar with the terminology. If you know that the audience is not, then you should take a moment to define technical terms.

How do you know if they are familiar with the words? Your earlier audience analysis will help you determine whether or not you will have to explain your word choices. If you are speaking about computer technology and everyone in the room is computer literate, then you probably won't have to explain too much of what you are saying. But if only 10 per cent of the audience are involved with computers, you may have to take time to explain what you mean when you discuss CPUs and megabytes.

How do you explain? You can give your explanations as you go along or you can provide a handout with significant terms to which you refer. You can use visuals. Don't forget, abbreviations should be explained as well. You may argue that you don't have enough time to make explanations. But if your audience doesn't understand what you mean, then it doesn't matter how much time you have – they won't understand your message.

WAY 32   WATCH FOR COLLOQUIALISMS

You have heard the phrase, 'global village' often enough. True, the world is smaller, and we have contact with people all over the planet. But we don't all speak the same language. As a speaker bear in mind that nowadays your audience may be filled with people from different parts of the country, of the continent, or of the world.

- A phrase you grew up using in the north may not be understood in the south.
- What you say in the city may not be commonly understood by someone from the country.
- An expression you learned from your parents may no longer be in use by a member of a younger generation.

Listen to any teenager for a few minutes. You will hear new

words that they have introduced into the language that you may not understand. So, when you review your talk, be sure that the phrases you are using are familiar to all your listeners.

WAY 33   LOOK FOR IDIOSYNCRASIES

Your word choices may come from your education or they may come from your specialization. Some other words that you use may just come from habit.

- Do you say 'you know' or 'right?' frequently when you are speaking?
- Do you say 'like' at the end of sentences?
- Do you have a pet word like 'absolutely' or 'marvellous' that you sprinkle around unnecessarily?

Whatever the word, try to notice it. Think if you have any pet phrases. Then catch yourself using them. If you use them too often, then try to eliminate them over time. Don't berate yourself if you hear yourself using 'irregardless' for the third time in a paragraph. Just decrease the number of repetitions.

What you don't want is for your audience to focus on your pet phrase. You want them to remember your message. Repetition increases the odds of someone retaining your words. Well, sometimes you don't want some phrases retained.

Eight
Notes

Some people feel that you look more professional if you speak off-the-cuff. The following four ways are meant to encourage you to think twice before you make the decision to avoid notes and to be a completely spontaneous speaker. Avoid reading. Use notes, preferably on cards and take advantage of the freedom that cards provide.

WAY 34   AVOID READING

Please don't read to your audience. True, there are times that you must 'deliver a paper' the way academics do. For the most part, though, the process is deadly dull for the audience. The truth is that they could read your paper at their leisure, get more out of it and be in more comfortable surroundings. If the audience knows that they can get a copy of what you are reading to them, they may not even listen to what you are saying when you are at the podium. The value of speaking instead of reading is that it allows you to react to what is happening around you.

Unless you have electronic equipment to aid you, there is another reason to avoid reading. When you read your eyes of necessity are focused on the paper in front of you. While you are reading, you can not see what is going on in the audience. You can not see if people are looking confused or tired. Furthermore, when you read you tilt your head down and your voice is projected down as well. Way 40 speaks about how vital eye-contact is for a good talk.

WAY 35   USE NOTES

Yes, you should have notes. Encouraging you not to read your talk doesn't mean that you should avoid using notes.

Besides giving you something to do with your hands, notes serve two basic purposes. First, they help stop you forgetting what you have planned to say. It can happen. Some people are so terrified in the opening minutes of a talk that they literally go blank. They remember nothing. I know. I have been there. Having notes means that you have something to fall back on should you suffer from such an attack of nerves that you can not continue. Such a level of anxiety rarely happens. It happened to me only once, and I didn't have notes. I learned a terrible lesson. Don't you do the same.

Second, notes are invaluable for the opposite condition – too much talking instead of too little. Some people begin to enjoy the sense of power over the audience. Such speakers go off on tangents and are natural storytellers. So they spontaneously recollect additional anecdotes or delight in interrupting their own presentations by providing lengthy answers to unasked questions. Such people can talk 30 minutes longer than scheduled with ease. Notes rein them in. They need notes to remind them of their original plans and to assist them in returning to them. No matter how enthralling your talk may be, audiences have other obligations.

WAY 36   CONSIDER USING CARDS

You may wonder if you are being given contradictory information. On the one hand you are being discouraged from reading, and on the other, you are being encouraged to use notes. What should you do? Use cards. Put your notes on 3 × 5 or 5 × 8 cards. Both are good sizes. The 3 × 5 cards fit neatly into a pocket.

Why should you use cards and what should you put on them?

When you use cards, you don't need a lectern on which to rest your papers. Cards allow you to keep your head up because you can bring your cards up rather than move your head down. You need only look down to check and then look up to speak. Thus, you can keep your eyes on the audience. With your head up, you can project your voice better. In addition, you can go on to the next card without the annoying rustling sound that sheets of paper can make.

Cards also allow you to practise anywhere with greater ease and flexibility. You can keep them in a pocket for easy access. You can take them out on the plane, the train, your office or in the hallway.

What should you put on the cards?

They are cue cards. They are prompts. You don't write out your talk on them. If you do, you risk reading again. First of all, number each card consecutively. It is easy for them to get mixed up. On each card, put one or two of your key ideas. Don't write it all out word-for-word. You may also want to write a key word or phrase like 'red car' or 'John's report' to remind you of the material you are going to use to support your argument. You can actually copy your slides on to your cards, too. If you anticipate being extremely nervous, then you may want to write out the entire first few sentences, or the names of significant people who need to be identified or thanked.

How many cards should you have?

There is no rule. You may have as few as five cards. Or as many as 50. Be patient with yourself. If you have never used cards before they take some adjustment. But once you get the feel of looking down, checking and then looking up to continue, you will discover that they give you both security and freedom.

WAY 37   USE THE SPACE

When you are using cards, you are better able to use the space around you. You can move. You can walk around. During a 10 or 15 minute talk or even a longer one, a speaker who moves around is more motivating to listeners and is also easier to pay attention to than a static figure. The audience pays attention. When you move closer to individuals or to sections of your audience, those individuals or groups become more attentive.

On the other hand, when you read a paper, you are glued to one spot because you have to put your papers on a table or on a lectern. If it is a lectern, the audience can only see your shoulders and your head, not your entire body. You may not be able to move much to the right or to the left. Your use of your hands is limited, because they are on the lectern or are turning pages. Unless you are very tall or have an adjustable stand on which to place your papers, you may be lost behind the box. Basically, the more fixed you are in one spot, the less interesting you are to your audience. The less interesting you are, the harder it is for the audience to concentrate for a long period on what you are saying.

Nine
Your Presence

Your physical appearance plays a significant part in the creation of a successful presentation. Certainly what you are saying is what matters to your listeners, but how you look and what you do when you are speaking can detract from or enhance your presence. Let's look at some ways to ensure success.

WAY 38   IMPROVE YOUR STANCE

For years you have probably been told to 'stand up straight and don't slouch'. Well, you are about to hear it again. One of the reasons for that recommendation is that standing up straight allows you to breathe more deeply, which is calming, and to project your voice more effectively. Another reason for standing tall is that you appear more confident.

Can you visualize speakers you have heard in the past?

- Some stand with one hip up and one shoulder down looking very much like a cowboy who has just ridden into town.
- Other speakers shift their weight back and forth from one leg to the other.
- Still others lean on the lectern or table in front of them or rock back and forth.
- Others rock up and back on their toes.

All of these movements detract from what you are saying because they, rather than your words, become the focus of the audience's attention.

Ideally when you are not moving around, stand with

your legs far enough apart to support your weight. Imagine drawing a line from your shoulders straight down; where the line touches the floor is where your feet should be. Stand with your feet about eight to ten inches apart – more if you are tall. The reason is that if you stand with your feet touching, you may find yourself rocking from side to side as if you were a tree being cut down or blown over by a high wind.

WAY 39 USE YOUR HEAD

Of course, you say, you have to 'use your head' if you are going to give a talk. But, literally use your head. Hold your head up and lift your chin. Look out toward your audience. Your head can be expressive. But remember that your head should be consistent with your words. There is no reason why you can not shake your head 'no' if you are saying something negative, or nod your head slightly when your remarks are positive. You do not have to hold your head stiffly if you are making a quizzical remark – you can tilt your head to the side.

This recommendation is not a suggestion to plan and rehearse all your head movements. This is a suggestion to use your head naturally, in exactly the same way as you would if you were engaged in a conversation with another person. In that situation, you would agree, disagree, think, appear pleased or quizzical simply by moving your head. Do the same when you speak to an audience of more than one.

WAY 40 EYES FRONT

The eyes have been called the 'windows of the soul'. They are also the keys to giving effective presentations. No matter how hard it is for you to look at the faces of your audience, you simply have to learn to look at them. Really look at them. See them. The only times you should take your eyes off them is when you are checking your cue cards, changing a slide or making some other technical move.

You look at the audience, and you look at everybody.

Move your eyes around the room. Look at those in the back. Look at the people in the front. Look at the people on the sides. Please do not talk to a window or over the heads of the audience the way many people do. Talk to the audience.

The reason that you are looking at the audience is to show them that you are earnest about what you are saying. In addition, you are looking at them to see how and if they are reacting to what you are telling them. Being aware of that second dimension is critical. You need to see how the audience is responding to what you are saying so that you can alter, emphasize, clarify or reinforce your point.

- If they are falling asleep, you may have to find a way to wake them up.
- If they look confused, you may have to repeat or clarify.
- If they look angry, you may have to anticipate some questions.

In other words, look at your audience, let them see your face and react to what you see them doing as you speak.

One caveat: be careful of focusing on a friend, a power figure or a 'nodder'. In you desire to please it is easy to direct your talk toward one person rather than the whole group. Catch yourself and look around the entire room. Even if most people are sitting in one section, look at the area where only a few are seated.

WAY 41   LOOK PLEASANT

Being advised to look pleasant may seem very silly to you. But once again, recall speakers you have heard. Many people have sour or sullen faces at the beginning of a talk and continue to look that way until the end. If you want your audience to react positively to what you are saying, your face, like your head, should mirror your words. If you are proud or enthusiastic about your message, then your face should look proud and enthusiastic. If you are concerned, look concerned. If you are amused, look amused. If you are startled, look startled.

Do smile. Some people think that presenting is such a serious business that you must look earnest. Smiling does not detract from the seriousness of your message. Of course, you have to be sensible. You don't smile when you are announcing lay-offs, budget freezes or other bad news, unless your motive is to be cynical and sinister. Do smile when what you are saying is upbeat and has positive implications for the people in front of you. The audience will like you more.

WAY 42   USE YOUR ARMS AND HANDS

Your arms and hands are both the most valuable and least expensive visuals that you have. Learn to take advantage of them. When you give a talk:

- Don't put one or both hands in your pockets.
- Don't put your hand in your pocket and play with your keys or your loose change.
- Don't put your hands behind your back.
- Don't fidget with pens and pencils.

Instead, please use your hands to make your points:

- Gesture with them.
- Show measurements with them.
- Heft the weight of an imaginary object.
- Demonstrate movements.

You can open your hands. You can close them. You can plead with them. You can be adamant with them. You can look open with them. You can punctuate or underline your ideas with them. In essence, use them in exactly the same way that you do when you are having a conversation.

Another caveat: please don't point at members of the audience. Pointing can appear to be either threatening or rude and is thus distracting. Beware of pointing not only with your finger, but also with a pen, pencil or pointer. Pounding the table is equally annoying, especially if you have an open microphone nearby.

WAY 43   WATCH FOR DISTRACTING GESTURES

As we just noted, pointing can be distracting. Other gestures may detract from your talk as well. Many of us have physical as well as verbal idiosyncrasies. Again, recall talks or lectures you have sat through during your lifetime.

- Can you recall speakers repeatedly smoothing the seats of their trousers or straightening their ties?
- Can you recall speakers who fiddled with a button, pulled down a hem or pulled up a bra strap?
- Can you recall speakers who repeatedly twisted a stray strand of hair around an ear, or stroked their own faces, wiped their brows or pushed their sliding glasses back up their noses?

All these gestures are perfectly normal. But each of them can become problematic when they are repeated too frequently. The audience begins to focus on the nervous idiosyncrasies rather than on listening to the import of your message.

WAY 44   MIND YOUR FEET

Don't assume that the audience is looking only at your face and hands. Unless you are hidden behind a lectern – and I hope you aren't – the audience will see all of you, from your head to your feet. In Way 38 you were encouraged to stand tall and plant your feet. As we said, unfortunately, many speakers rock back and forth on their toes. You may think no one will notice if you are standing behind a lectern. That isn't true. The audience can see your shoulders and head rise and fall every time you rock.

- Some speakers appear to be practising dance steps.
- Still others look like new ice-skaters whose ankles keep bending.
- Some speakers slip their feet in and out of their shoes.

- Others try to polish their shoes by rubbing them against the back of their trousers.

Nothing wrong with any of these behaviours as such, unless they are so frequent or creative that the audience becomes more intrigued by your foot movements than by your recommendations for change.

WAY 45   CONSIDER MOVING

You have been encouraged to stand erect and look out at the audience. You can be even more interesting and powerful as a speaker if you move around. You are more interesting to watch and to listen to when you move. You can motivate people to pay attention if you change position.

What kind of movement? If you are on a dais, you can walk to the left or to the right of where you originally started speaking. You can walk toward a corner of the room. You can move closer to some members of the audience. You can move up an aisle or down the side. When you do, your proximity may actually cause some people to feel mildly uncomfortable as you approach. But they concentrate again. Don't get so close that you are invading someone's personal space. Just get close enough to encourage them to refocus their attention on you.

When you move, you aren't pacing like a caged animal, nor are you marching about like an irate schoolmaster ready to catch someone for reading a comic instead of a history book. You are moving so that everyone can see and hear you and to create some additional interest.

Ten
Your Clothing

How you choose to dress for a talk is important. Remember that your audience looks at the whole person when you stand up, are introduced or walk to the front of the room. What you are wearing forms part of an impression.

WAY 46 CHOOSE YOUR HAIRSTYLE

Let's look at your hair. Some of you may think that this recommendation is directed only toward women. It is not. It is for men and women.

Earlier we said that maintaining eye-contact is essential to giving a successful talk.

- If you have hair combed over one eye or constantly falling over your eyes, you can not maintain eye-contact.
- If you have hair with a mind of its own that prefers to fall over your face and ears and you find yourself trying to put it back behind your ears, that gesture is distracting.
- If you are frequently swishing your head back like a horse tossing its mane, you are creating a distraction.

In essence, when you give a talk, choose a hairstyle that allows the audience to see your face. You don't want them spending time admiring your wonderful mane of hair, marvelling that it has a life of its own and ignoring your ideas.

WAY 47 YOUR SHOES

First of all, look to see if your shoes are scuffed or are worn down at the heels. If they are, please clean or shine them or have them re-heeled. With polished shoes you look more professional. You also look as if you cared about your appearance and care about what the audience thinks.

Pick shoes that have no idiosyncrasies of their own. Some shoes love to squeak when you wear them. Others have wayward laces that enjoy becoming untied. Others have hard soles and make a noise as you walk to the podium or around the area.

Pick shoes that are comfortable. You are going to be on your feet for a while when you give a talk or field questions. Select shoes that don't hurt your feet after 15 minutes. All this may sound obvious, but it is surprising how people inadvertently make the daunting task of speaking even harder by letting small details undermine them.

WAY 48   SELECT YOUR OUTFIT

Plan ahead. Don't wake up on the morning of a talk and discover that you have only one clean outfit to wear. Pick the one that you are going to wear in advance and be sure that it is clean and in good repair:

- Check to see that hems of skirts, trousers or jackets are not coming undone or have a wayward thread dangling down.
- Look for loose or missing buttons.
- Inspect for frayed collars, pockets or cuffs.
- Double-check for that soup stain on the front of a tie or blouse.
- Be sure that a pen hasn't leaked in your pocket.

Decide on an outfit that is appropriate for the occasion. Usually something simple or tailored is better. Ask yourself if the pattern on the tie you selected is more interesting than what you are planning to say. If you are a woman ask yourself if your 2-inch earrings and décolletage are appropriate for this event or whether something less dramatic might be wiser for the occasion.

Choose clothes that fit you. You don't need your collar to be too big for your neck. You don't need your trouser cuffs gathering at your ankles or your sleeves sliding down those invaluable hands of yours. You don't need to wear socks that slide down under your heel or to have ladders in your tights.

Choose a combination of colours that you believe is effective. Dark against light gives you the greatest contrast and therefore the greatest appearance of authority. If that is not the image that you want to project, then choose a softer combination, such as beige and blue. But make the decision in advance. Don't let what is clean and pressed in your wardrobe on the morning of your talk dictate your choice for you.

Eleven
Your Voice

Let's talk about your voice. Many speakers underestimate the importance of their vocal quality. In fact, most of us don't take full advantage of what that remarkable instrument can do to enhance a presentation. The way you use your voice can make your talk more interesting. As we said before, the more dynamic your talk, the more likely it is that your audience will be able to concentrate on you and on your message.

WAY 49   ADJUST YOUR SPEED

As you know we are capable of speaking rapidly and slowly. We can also speak at a pace somewhere in between those two. Do so. Throughout your talk, vary the pace at which you speak. If you stay at one pace all the way through then your talk becomes monotonous for the listeners. Speed up through sections or sentences that may not be as essential to your central point. Slow down through more difficult passages or more important sections. You decide when and where.

Remember, most of us speak more rapidly at the beginning of a talk than we do later because we are more nervous when we begin. Thus when you say your opening sentences, you should make a concerted effort to slow yourself down.

By the way, suppose you know that you have a strong regional accent or you are speaking to a group whose native language is not your own. You should make an effort to ensure that everyone can understand you. The best way to do that is to slow down.

WAY 50   ADJUST THE VOLUME

Think of yourself as a stereo system. You can adjust the volume. You can speak loudly sometimes and softly at other times. If you speak at the same volume all the time, you become as monotonous as if you were speaking at the same speed all the time.

Know your own voice. If you have a big voice and you find yourself working in an intimate setting, your talk can become overbearing. Sometimes lowering the volume so that you speak softly causes people to lean forward and pay more attention. There is no rule that says you have to request a microphone. But, if you do use one, ask for a clip-on that allows you freedom of movement. Then speak naturally.

WAY 51   CHECK FOR EXTRANEOUS SOUNDS

It is always good to record yourself once or twice on a cassette so that you can play it back and listen to yourself. What should you pay attention to? Listen not only for the quality of the talk. Also listen for sounds you make without realizing that you do. Sometimes we think out loud, so:

- Listen for 'ems' and 'ers'.
- Listen for lip smacking sounds, too.
- Listen for 'tsk'.

Some people press their tongues against the roofs of their mouths and then pull them away. That action creates a kissing sound. Please understand that there is nothing inherently wrong with saying 'em' or 'er' or 'tsk'. But like so much of presenting, at some point the sounds can become a distraction. If you hear yourself making them you should seriously consider eliminating them. They are just like extraneous gestures. The audience becomes more focused on the sound or gesture than on the message you want to share.

WAY 52   BE YOURSELF

Speak naturally. Speak in a conversational tone. Yes, most of us would be delighted if we sounded like Judi Dench, Anthony Hopkins, or Kenneth Brannagh in Shakespearean roles. There is no need. You are not there to give sermons or soliloquies to the assembled masses. You are there to convince your colleagues of the merits of your arguments or recommendations. While it is true that much of presentation is theatrical, there is no need to intone or pontificate. Speak like a colleague. However, that doesn't mean that you should be so relaxed and casual that you are not in charge of how you sound or what you say.

WAY 53   PAUSE

One of the most effective ways of bringing home a point is by pausing. Pausing means actually stopping in your tracks and waiting. For most of us this is hard to do. We are uncomfortable with silence. But, if you pause, you allow your audience time to absorb your words or to reflect on what you have said or what you have shown them.

How do you pause? Simply come to the end of a thought and wait. Pausing throughout your talk after key sections is effective. *You* decide when is a good time.

There is one time when you should always stop and pause and that is at the end of a talk. The pause should follow your last sentence. Make your final remark. Wait. Then change your head or posture or your tone of voice. Then thank your audience or prepare to take questions. There should be a clear differentiation between your presentation and the closing amenities. Don't let your farewell interfere with your closing statements. Your powerful message may get lost.

WAY 54   BE ENTHUSIASTIC

Think about it. If you don't care about the subject matter of your talk, why should your colleagues? Whatever your topic and no matter how often you may have had to say what you are saying, you should sound fresh and enthusiastic. Presumably your words are new to your audience. Earlier we suggested that your face should look pleasant; well, your voice should sound it too. You can put a smile in your voice.

Next time you make a telephone call, listen to the way the person answers. It isn't just the words they say. Listen to the tone of voice. Some people sound as if they can barely make it through the day. Others sound as if they resent the interruption. Still others sound as if they are pleased to be at work and even more delighted to be hearing from you.

When you give a presentation you can and should sound enthusiastic or committed to your subject matter regardless of what it is that you are trying to explain to your audience. Be interested in your subject. If you are, the odds are that your audience will be too.

Even if they are having bad days, actors have to care as much about their performances on the fiftieth night as on opening night. We do, too. Trainers who have taught a course a number of times, or individuals who run induction meetings know that they need to sound as if the material is new and exciting. If they don't, the audience will be less motivated.

Twelve
Your Nerves

Most people are terrified of being terrified. But there are techniques that may help you to alleviate some of the anxiety. Let's look at some of the ways.

WAY 55   WELCOME STAGE FRIGHT

Stage fright is normal. Actors experience pounding hearts. Musicians face sweaty palms. Athletes have dry throats. No matter what you call it, 'the jitters', 'butterflies' or 'stage fright' are perfectly normal experiences. Your adrenaline is flowing. Sometimes after an injection at the dentist's, you may notice that your hands shake and your heart races. You are experiencing an 'adrenaline rush'. When you do, you are more alert and ready to take on your opponent, to face the music and the audience. If you think about it, you realize that the anxious feeling does not last very long. It is the unusual person who is on edge throughout an entire talk.

If you think about the last time you spoke before a group or got ready to take part in some kind of competition, the adrenaline flowed and got you going. Then your talent, technique and preparation got you through the rest. You are nervous because you want to do well. You want to survive. You want a positive reception. You don't want to appear foolish. But usually within a minute or two of the beginning your heart stops racing and your hands stop shaking as you move into your prepared remarks. The beginning of a talk is when you are most worried. It is healthy and normal. What is helpful is to recognize your own patterns of nervousness. We tend to be nervous in our own individual ways.

WAY 56   KNOW YOUR HABITS

We do not experience nervousness in exactly the same way as each other. For some, their mouths go dry. For others, hands shake or the palms of their hands become wet. Still others experience a flush. For others their stomachs feel rocky – the famous butterflies. Still others feel weakness in their legs. Get to know your own body and anticipate what you feel when you are nervous. Depending on how your nervousness manifests itself, there are ways of handling or overcoming it:

- If your mouth goes dry, have a glass of room-temperature water nearby to sip.
- If your hands shake, then have your materials prepared, so you are not reaching for notes, pens or slides in the opening seconds of your talk. Be sure to keep your hands away from the tray on which you place transparencies. Your shaking hands will be magnified and projected on to the screen.
- If your stomach feels hollow, be sure that you avoid any caffeinated drinks before your talk. Frankly, that advice is true for all speakers. Caffeine, as you well know, heightens the jitters and acts as a diuretic. The latter may send you running to the loo when you have other more pressing concerns, like presenting your talk.
- If your legs feel weak, be sure that you know the route to the front of the room or be already sitting there when it is your turn to speak. You don't need to trip up a flight of steps because your legs are not working the way they normally do.
- Take some good deep breaths to calm yourself.

In other words, no matter how often you speak, you will always experience some degree of stage fright. That anxiety will manifest itself in particular ways for you. Whatever that way is, expect it and compensate for it.

WAY 57   HANDLE MISTAKES AND SURPRISES

Mistakes happen. We are human after all. We lose our place. We misspeak. We skip a sentence. We use the wrong name or word. The slide jams or the Power Point goes down. The microphone goes off. A flex is pulled out of the wall. Someone comes in a wrong door. You can list even more human or technical glitches.

What is important is that you try to take the slip in your stride. Don't try to hide it, to cover it up and pretend that it didn't happen. Deal with the problem. Make the correction. Ask for a moment to correct it, if it is a technical problem. Smile. Joke, if you can. Don't blame anyone else. Everyone in the room has been in the same situation. Frankly, if you handle the problem well, you will enchant the audience. They will see you as more human and more credible.

That last remark is not suggesting that you deliberately make mistakes to win their approval, but if a problem does arise, address it, don't try to hide. By the way, one or two mistakes are accepted. But when errors occur too often, you alienate the audience. What appears to be an inadvertent slip-up suddenly becomes lack of preparation, and the audience does not appreciate the lack of effort on their behalf.

WAY 58   DEVELOP STRATEGIES

In addition to developing coping mechanisms for your nervousness, like having water nearby or avoiding coffee, you can think of other ways of handling your nerves.

- You can write your opening remarks on a card. That way if you are extremely anxious, you have prompts. You can read from your written words while your heart beat slows down.
- You can have your materials ready, so that all you have to do is push a button to start your slide or video, pick up your first transparency or reach for your marker.

- You can take the focus off yourself at the beginning by asking the audience a question.
- You can change the focus by immediately turning to write something on the flip-chart or overhead. The audience will think about the question or look at the flip-chart rather than your hands.
- You can have material 'pre-flipped', so that all you have to do is turn a page.
- You can give the audience something to read.

Given the unique nature of your talk, you may be able to create your own techniques. Experiment. But remember that what works for someone else may not work for you. The reverse is also true.

WAY 59   BE SENSIBLE

We have already said that you should be careful about drinking caffeinated drinks before you give a talk, because they heighten anxiety. Those of you who don't like to fly are advised to do the same thing for the same reason. But avoiding caffeine doesn't mean avoiding food. Eat. Don't go into a talk without having eaten something. You don't need to feel light-headed or headachy because you have skipped breakfast or lunch. On the other hand, don't overeat. Avoid heavy, greasy foods. What you don't need when you are speaking is to belch or to have indigestion.

Some people want to drink alcohol or take medication to calm down. You don't have the same kind of control of yourself when you do. Instead:

- Take deep breaths. Let the oxygen calm your system.
- Think happy thoughts, as Peter Pan admonished us to do.
- Use relaxation techniques.
- Visualize calm images. Think of peaceful scenes.

Right now, think of a place that is quiet for you. It may be an empty seashore or a meadow of flowers or a furze-covered hillside. Find the image that is calming for you and recall it before you have to give your talk.

WAY 60   BE POSITIVE

One of the best ways of overcoming your nervousness is to remind yourself that you have something useful to share with the audience. You can spend time listening to voices in your head telling you that you are going to make a mistake, that you are going to trip or forget what you had planned to say. Instead, say to yourself that what you have to say can make a difference to the people in front of you. Your ideas can affect their lives or their work. Perhaps what you say will:

- save money or time;
- make the audience feel better about themselves;
- make them laugh or smile;
- clarify or eliminate confusion;
- help them know more than they did before.

Regardless of what you are planning to say to the audience, before you begin remind yourself that you have something useful to say. That message to yourself reassures a failing ego or a weakened sense of self-esteem.

Thirteen
The Arena or Stage

Because many of you may feel that your talk is a 'me against them' contest, some of you may think of the venue as an arena. Some may consider the presentation as a theatrical event, so they think of the venue as a stage. Regardless of the name, it is the place where you will speak. The more you know about it, the more effective you will be as a speaker.

WAY 61   GET ACQUAINTED WITH THE LAYOUT

One of the best ways to overcome your fear and to give an effective presentation is to investigate the room in which you will be working. Visit the room in advance. All you need is a few minutes. If the location is far away, fly in early. If it is in another building, make arrangements to visit. If it is in your own offices, stop by early in the morning. But do visit the room. Walk around. Study it from all angles. Ask questions like:

- Where will I be sitting?
- Where will the audience be sitting?
- Where will I be speaking?
- What is the walk like from my seat to the podium?
- Will I stand up from my seat to speak?
- Can everyone see me?
- How far am I from my audience?
- Will the audience be too comfortable on soft chairs or uncomfortable on metal seats?
- Do the chairs squeak?
- Are the floors carpeted, concrete or wooden?

- Where are the windows?
- Where are the doors?
- Can people come in and out?
- Are there telephone extensions in the room? Will they ring?
- Are there wires on the floor? Can I or others trip over them?
- How is the audience arranged?
- Is there a lectern?
- Do I have to walk up or down any steps?

Be sure to survey the room so that you can anticipate any potential problems.

WAY 62   CHECK THE ACOUSTICS

When you do your walk about, check for the quality of the sound. Are there heavy curtains on the windows? Is the room heavily carpeted? If so, then you know that sound will be absorbed. If you find that the room is bare and the floors uncovered, then you may have an echo. Sometimes if you walk on a wooden floor your footsteps will make more noise than you want. Look up as well as down:

- Is the ceiling high?
- Will your voice be lost?
- What is on the other side of the wall?
- Are the walls thick? Are they temporary walls?
- What is scheduled next door? Are noises next door or in the area going to interrupt your talk? Will the sounds of an exuberant activity come through the walls?

Be sure that your audience will not be distracted and that they can hear you. What you learn will help you determine if you need to amplify your voice.

WAY 63   DETERMINE YOUR NEEDS

Once you have walked around like a detective, then decide what you need to adjust and what you need to request. In addition to surveying the room, speak to the back and decide if you need a mike or not. In a boardroom, it is unlikely that you will, but in a large conference room you might.

- Do you need flip-charts, tables, screens or over-heads? Are they already there?
- Is the flip-chart on the correct side for you, depending on whether you are right- or left-handed?
- If you are bringing your own equipment will you need extension cords, markers, erasers, transparencies? Will they be there waiting for you? Have you asked for them?
- If you are projecting slides or films, what are you projecting on? Will the screen be down? Is it a pull-down screen? Can you reach it? Is it hand-pulled or does it operate electronically?
- Where are the switches for lights, for projectors?
- Do you need a table for your materials? Is it the right size for you to put your materials on?
- Does the room get dark enough? Are there blinds? Could you see your own notes if all the lights were out?

In other words, once you have looked around the area in which you will be working, determine what you will need to ensure that the presentation runs smoothly.

Fourteen
Practising

Most of us have had to practise at some time in our lives. If we sang, played an instrument or were involved in a sport, we had to practise. While many of us may not have liked the routine of the exercises, scales or drills, we knew we had to do them. What we wanted was to get on with the singing, the playing or the competing. But we knew that practise did make a difference in our performances. It is no different for speaking.

WAY 64   BUILD CONFIDENCE

Practising builds your confidence. If you are more confident, not only will you appear more sure of yourself, you will also be less nervous. Practising for a talk consists of running through the talk to increase your familiarity with it and saying it out loud a number of times. Even if you only have time for two or three run-throughs, each time you say it, you become more at ease with your own words. In addition, you may want to make some changes in the content.

- You may see opportunities for emphasis or for pausing.
- You may sense that sections drag or need to be cut a bit.
- You may want to keep certain material, but you decide to speak quickly when you go over that particular section.
- You may discover that you want to include a thought, an analogy or a story that you hadn't thought of before.

Those changes, the decisions about delivery and your

growing familiarity with your material, increases your sense of security. Remember you are not committing your talk to memory. In fact, please don't! You lose spontaneity when you do. But do know your talk well enough, so that you become less reliant on your notes. You want your note cards to be cue cards not a script.

WAY 65   CHECK THE TIME

When you practise, check your timing. Look at your watch or a clock when you start, then periodically as you speak and again when you finish. If you are scheduled to speak for 30 minutes, your talk should run slightly under 30 minutes, not longer. If you see that you are running over time, then you will have to make some adjustments.

Earlier we urged you to practise your talk aloud. The reason is that we don't read silently at the same pace that we read aloud. Certainly reading to yourself increases your familiarity with your material, but reading aloud permits you to take pauses, to talk quickly or to slow down.

As you practise, imagine the audience reacting to what you are saying. You need to plan for those reactions. Build in time for a laugh. If you are using visuals, allow time for the audience to look at what you are showing them. If you see that you are running over time in your rehearsal, you may consider eliminating some of your material – a decision that is better made beforehand than on the day.

WAY 66   LIMIT MISTAKES

The more you practise, the fewer mistakes you will make. No, don't anticipate making hundreds of mistakes when you present. You may make one or two, or none. When you practise with your notes, when you listen to yourself, when you become increasingly more comfortable with what comes first or second, – it is only then that you don't have to ask yourself, 'What do I say next?' The segues will come more naturally.

In addition, you will be able to time yourself and to be less concerned and more at ease with what you are doing. If you have a difficult section to deliver, you have the opportunity to run through that part several times just as you would within a difficult passage in music, or an awkward move in sports. One reason for practising is to increase your comfort level with your material, thus limiting your mistakes and freeing you to concentrate on the audience's behaviour, not on your own.

WAY 67   WORK IN THE ROOM

In addition to walking around the venue, arrange time to practise in the room. Up to now you may have been practising in your office, in the bathroom, in a corridor, or in your living room. Now try to practise in the room you are going to be using. As you did when you evaluated it in advance, now arrange to come in early or schedule a time with the organizers or the person who called the meeting to get into the room and practise. It doesn't matter if chairs are being set up while you are in there, just do your thing. All you need is five minutes to survey and then enough time to run through your talk once.

- Get used to where you will be standing.
- Determine whether or not there is room to walk around.
- Check the sight lines to determine if everyone can see you from every seat.
- Check the lighting to see if there is any glare or if you can read your notes.
- See if blinds, curtains or shades need to be adjusted slightly to allow you to see the audience or for them to see your projected material.
- Sit in one of the audience's seats. Shift your weight around in it. Listen for noise.
- Test your voice by going to the front and saying a sentence or two while someone stands in the back. Ask if you can be heard. Remember that when the room is filled you will have to speak more loudly.
- Discover if the room has any idiosyncrasies like columns, a noisy ventilation system, or a squeaking floor board where you are standing.

- See if the equipment you requested has been set up and is working.
- Be sure that the flip-chart has enough paper and is located where you want it positioned.
- Check that you have the right type and colour of markers for the flip-chart or for the board.

Although you may feel silly, give your talk in the room even if the room is empty. Move around. Check your watch from time to time. A dress rehearsal makes a difference.

WAY 68   KNOW YOUR EQUIPMENT

Not only should you know your flip-charts:, be sure that you know any electric or electronic equipment that you are working with, even if it is your own. You are a pilot checking your instruments before take-off. Depending on what you are using, make your own mental check list. It might include:

- Being sure that no one has borrowed a piece of equipment that you need.
- Double-checking for the location of power switches.
- Checking the extension cords.
- Testing the microphone.
- Making sure the light goes on if you are using the overhead projector.
- Removing any dust or stray hairs from lenses.
- Being sure that TV monitors are set to the correct channel.
- Rewinding tapes.
- Testing your computer.

Be sure that your equipment is placed in the right location so that any images that you are projecting fit clearly and neatly on the screen. You don't want legs cut off, or the last bullet point in a list projected on the wall below the screen. Sadly, good talks fall down because technical interruptions occur that could have been avoided with a few minutes of preparation.

Fifteen
Questions

Sometimes you can give a talk and it is all in one direction – from you to the audience. More often than not, however, your talk involves some exchange of ideas. That dialogue takes the form of questions. Therefore, a good presenter recognizes that it is essential to prepare both for the formal talk and for questions.

WAY 69   ANTICIPATE QUESTIONS

Probably the best way to prepare for any questions or for a formal question-and-answer session is to think about your audience once again. Remind yourself who will be present. Think again about their personalities and their job titles. When you do, you will begin to put yourself in their shoes and think from their perspectives. Depending on your subject ask yourself some questions. Having heard your message, will people be concerned:

- About cost?
- About safety?
- About time-frames?
- About perceptions?
- About the long-term implications?
- About ease of access?
- About training?
- About the personnel that will be needed?

In other words, consider how what you are planning to say might affect members of your audience or the people they represent.

As you anticipate some of their questions, you can begin

to formulate some of your answers. In some instances you may want to build some of your answers into your talk. You do that by saying something like, 'Some of you may be wondering how we can implement such recommendations…' or, 'You may be concerned by the costs associated with this project, therefore…'. In addition to anticipating questions yourself, you may prefer to have some questions posed by someone else – a colleague who will listen to your rehearsal and be willing to challenge your ideas.

WAY 70   LISTEN

To answer questions well, you need to listen to what is being asked of you. You don't want to cut off the questioner by answering before he or she has finished. In other words, don't finish the other person's sentence before he or she is done. Just stand there. Look at the individual and let the person pose the question. If what you are being asked is unclear, you may want to ask for clarification. You can say, 'Do I understand you to mean…?' or some similar phrase. Remember that your responses are part of your presentation as well. So listen intently and politely.

You should also be sure that everyone in the room hears the question. You can either ask the person to repeat the question for the group, or you can repeat the question yourself and answer it. You can say, 'Sam just asked if we will be…'. Then give your answer to the room, not just to the person who asked.

Sometimes an MC is identified who fields the questions for you. In that instance, you simply wait for the MC to identify the questioner and handle the questions in the same way that you would if no MC were there.

WAY 71   ANSWER

When you are asked a question, answer it. Certainly in political debates we see politicians avoid awkward questions by restating their positions or by attacking a member of another party. But in most instances in business there is no need to use such strategies. If you have the answer to the question, respond in an honest, straightforward manner. When you do, you will gain the respect of the audience.

If you don't know the answer, if you don't have the figures at hand, or if you don't have the necessary data with you, say so. Your professionalism and credibility are on the line. Presumably you have put a good deal of time and effort into delivering a quality talk. It would be a shame if you were to damage yourself by 'waffling', lying or making up statistics. We are not omniscient. Tell the questioners that you don't know the answer, or that you don't have the material with you. You can always provide it. By the way, if you do promise to send the material to them, be sure that you do.

If you are not sure of a particular answer, there are times when you can turn to a colleague who has worked with you on the project and whom you know may recollect the specific data. But beware of putting someone else on the spot.

WAY 72   STAY CALM

There are times and any number of reasons why members of the audience may irritate you:

- They may ask questions that you think are unreasonable.
- They may be using the meeting as a forum for their own personal agendas.
- They may be trying to posture in front of someone else.
- They may want to appear invaluable.
- They may want to appear intelligent.
- They may be trying to show someone else up – or you for that matter.

Hard as it may be to do under these circumstances, stay calm. Usually what happens is that the people asking such tough, provocative or awkward questions undermine themselves in the eyes of the audience. Instead of seeming clever, they appear arrogant. Thus, the question backfires and the questioners end up seeming pompous, petulant or impertinent. Don't underestimate the awareness of the audience – they recognize what is happening. When you are gracious, when you are patient, when you are charming, the other person looks foolish. Thus, there is no need for you to get into a shouting match. If need be, learn from political leaders. Take the high ground and repeat your stated position.

WAY 73 REMEMBER YOUR MAIN POINT

During a question-and-answer session it is easy to find yourself being asked tangential questions. Before long, you may realize that you have strayed far from your topic. It happens because one person poses a question, someone else picks up on that question, and then a third adds a follow-up. Before long you may find yourself far afield being asked questions that are no longer relevant to your topic.

If that happens, take charge. To return to your subject, you ask the audience if they have any questions about a particular aspect of what you were saying. In other words, you redirect the questions. Take the audience back to your message. Keep your original purpose in mind. Remember what you are trying to recommend or encourage and bring your answers back to that message. It is important for you to stay focused and not allow yourself to relax just because the formal part of the talk is over.

WAY 74 RESPECT THE QUESTIONER

Asking questions is a form of mini-presentation. All eyes move away from the speaker and to the person asking the question. Think about it. When you attend a meeting or a conference and are asked if you have any questions, you spend time formulating your question. Quite simply:

- You don't want to ask a stupid question.
- You don't want to ask a question that has already been asked.

- You don't want to ask a question that has been answered in the presentation.
- You don't want to appear as if you haven't been listening.

Those kinds of thoughts are going on in the minds of most questioners. You, as the speaker, should respect that anxiety. So, when you are asked questions, respect the people who ask them. They, not you, may be nervous now. Listen intently. Smile. Look pleased. If it is a thoughtful question, don't hesitate to say so. In other words, respect any person who has the courage to ask you a question. You will win them and their colleagues over.

Sixteen
Time

Among the variables that contribute to creating a good presentation, as we have indicated before, time is one of the most important. It is a precious commodity for us all. You should value your audience's time as well as your own.

WAY 75 REMEMBER YOU CAN SAY 'NO'

We have already said that making presentations is a daunting prospect for most of us. We fear for our reputations. That healthy anxiety is why you should never forget that if you are asked to present, you can say 'No'. Certainly one reason for declining is because you don't feel confident enough about the topic. However, it is unlikely that you would be asked to speak on a subject if you weren't viewed as knowledgeable.

Therefore, the main reason for saying 'No' is the realization that you don't have enough time to prepare for a good talk. Of course, in crisis situations you may have little or no choice. But when you are asked to speak to a conference, at a seminar or to a meeting, before you jump at the opportunity for visibility think twice about whether or not you have enough time to prepare adequately. You need time to prepare the content, to design the visuals and to practise. Therefore, if you feel that you can not do justice to your topic, your company or yourself, either decline the invitation or negotiate for a better time. Be realistic about what you can or can not do well.

WAY 76 ESTABLISH PARAMETERS

If you do decide to say 'Yes' to giving the presentation, then ask some more questions. Besides determining the date of the presentation, find out how long your talk is supposed to be. Is it to be 30 minutes or 15 minutes? If you are told you are to speak for 30 minutes, ask if that 30 minutes includes questions or whether the questions are additional. If the question period follows your 30-minute talk, then agree on how long that question period will be. You want to plan for the exact amount of time that you have. Don't settle for an answer like 'Oh, about 20 minutes or so' or 'around 30'. Many organizers are casual in their responses. For your own planning, you should know exactly how much time you have. On the day, you don't want to find yourself with too much or too little time.

WAY 77   KEEP YOUR WORD

You have been there. You have sat through talks that have gone on much longer than you expected. You were led to believe you'd be listening to a five-minute analysis, and 20 minutes later the individual is still on the podium talking. You don't want to run over time. That's why as a speaker you should wear a watch or have a clock within sight. That is also why you practise your talk. You want to come in on schedule.

People in the audience have expectations. They also have other responsibilities. If you say that you are going to spend the next five minutes explaining, then be sure that it is five minutes, not 10. If you begin by indicating that in '20 minutes, all of you will feel more comfortable with…', you have set up expectations for the audience. They expect 20 minutes, not 15 and certainly not 25. Keep your word. The audience will appreciate your sensitivity to their obligations. They will concentrate. They will also stay in their seats. You don't need people getting up to go. People leaving a room while someone is speaking is disruptive for everyone.

WAY 78   CONSIDER THE IMPLICATIONS

When you are asked to give a talk, think about when that talk is to be. Think about the time of the day, the time of the week and the time of the year. In other words, if you are asked to speak at 10 in the morning, more than likely your delivery would be different from a talk you might give at 8 in the evening. You might need to be more energetic at night, because people are more tired after a day's work.

The same is true for different days of the week. A talk given on a Monday morning is different in style from one given on Wednesday at 11am or one given on a Friday at 4:30pm. On Monday, people are refocusing from the weekend, and on Friday the weekend is beginning to return to their thoughts.

Consider too, what else is happening in the office or in the world:

- Are you scheduled to speak at the same time as a major sporting event, election or impending holiday? Is it the World Cup or a bank holiday?
- Are people more concerned with a rugby final than they are with what you have to say?
- Are you competing with people's attention for holiday parties?

So, think about the 'when' before you accept the offer to speak. If you do opt to present even though there is a major event happening simultaneously, recognize that you may have to modify your presentation style based on what that conflict or event is. In other words, consider all the implications of your time slot.

Seventeen
Conferences

Many times you will be speaking to small groups in your office, at a meeting with a client, or in your own board room. However, there will be times when you have to speak to a large group at a conference. What follows are some ways to increase your effectiveness in those situations.

WAY 79   PICK YOUR SLOT

It's wonderful to be invited to speak. You have been identified as someone with something to say. Remember that sometimes the organizers are more concerned with their own jobs, not yours. So beware of being so flattered by the honour of being approached that you allow yourself to be railroaded into being scheduled randomly by the organizers.

When you are invited to speak, be sure that you negotiate for the best slot for yourself. Don't accept what is given to you unless it is a time that works for you. For example, if you know that you are someone who is more alert in the morning than in the afternoon, then request an early slot. Conversely, if you know that you are more alert in the afternoon, ask for time in the afternoon. Don't be bashful. Remember you are a useful commodity for the organizer. It is in your best interests to make the request.

Before you agree to speak right after lunch, consider such a time slot well. Some people actually call it the 'black hole'. One reason for that name is that lunches at conferences are usually heavy-going. People may be sleepy. They may have been socializing over dessert and are reluctant to give up their opportunity to chat with new-found colleagues.

Either way they may not be too attentive. If you do agree to speak after lunch, design your talk accordingly. You may have to liven or lighten up your talk. In other words, your time slot and its relationship to other speakers is important for you to know.

WAY 80   CONSIDER OTHER SPEAKERS

If you are speaking at a conference, there will be other speakers. Find out who they are and when they will speak.

Find out the name of the keynote speaker, if it isn't you. Find out when he or she will be speaking and decide whether or not you want to precede or follow him or her. While not all of them are exciting speakers, some, because of who they are, can be. You certainly don't want to be viewed as a warm-up act or worse yet as an afterthought to the highlight of the day.

Find out what the keynote speaker and the others are going to be talking about. You need to know their subjects. You don't want to discover that you will be saying something similar to or contradictory to someone else on the day. You want to learn these things in advance so that you can prepare your remarks accordingly.

WAY 81   LISTEN AND MODIFY

By all means, on the day, try to arrange to listen to the other speakers, certainly to the ones ahead of you and if possible to those who follow. You may not be able to rearrange your schedule, but do try to hear the people who precede you. It is valuable for you to hear what other people say so that you can modify your own thoughts. When you listen to other speakers:

- You may find that someone is opposed to your notions and is contradicting everything you plan to say.
- You may find that someone has a similar position on one aspect of your talk.
- You may find that someone is dead wrong about something.

- You may find that someone uses a clever approach that charms the audience.

If you listen and think about your own talk, you may find that you can make minor adjustments or take advantage of what you have heard to enhance your own talk. There is no reason why you can't say, 'Despite my colleague's enthusiasm for...', 'I want to express my delight that John said...' or, 'Phyllis' reference to traffic reminds me of...'. You are showing that you listen and are also using the other speakers' words to reinforce or underline your own message.

Eighteen
Team Presentations

Most of what we have been discussing is solo meetings. Let's have a look at those other times when you will be asked or want to speak as part of a team with several of your colleagues. Preparing for such events is slightly different from working as a lone speaker.

WAY 82   PLAN TOGETHER

For a team presentation to appear professional and seamless, all of you should work together. Once you know what your topic is, you should discuss among yourselves who in the group will handle which section. In your deliberations:

- Decide if one of you is stronger in an area or if one of you is new to the material.
- Decide who will speak for how long.
- Decide who will speak first.
- Decide who will make the introductions.

You might also consider which one of you will assist with any technical materials you plan to use. For example, do flip-chart pages need to be turned? Would it be easier if someone else changed the transparencies on the overhead projector? Could one of your colleagues switch the computer on or click for the next slide? Rather than the speaker handling the technology, one of the team could be responsible until it is his or her turn to speak.

Another item to plan together is the handling of questions. Perhaps one of you wants to answer all of them. Or maybe you want to divide the subject matter into sections and have the person who spoke on that subject answer the questions relating to it. Again be sure to find the time to meet and divide the tasks.

WAY 83   PRACTISE TOGETHER

Just as you would do if you were performing alone, as a member of a team you should find the time to work in the room together. It looks bad when a group looks at each other anxiously, trying to make spontaneous decisions about what to do next. The decisions should have been made earlier:

- You should know where you are going to be seated or be standing.
- You should know how you are going to get to your places.

Determine how you are going to introduce your colleague without using the hackneyed expression, 'Now, I will hand it over to…'. Find a more creative and integrated way of moving to the next speaker: 'Ethel will now clarify why…', 'Stephen will walk you through the findings'.

Once again, the presentation should look like a package: smooth and wrapped up. If the first person began the talk with a question, the final speaker should recall that question. In essence, your opening phraseology or approach should be echoed in the ending. If you decide to develop a mnemonic, it should be used throughout the talk, not just by speaker number two.

Practising together increases your awareness of your differing styles. Thus you will be able to pace yourselves and alter your individual sections to complement each other.

WAY 84   PRESENT TOGETHER

'Of course, we will present together', you say. We are talking about *team* presentations. It is remarkable, though, how often team presentations still look like individual presentations given one right after another. If you are a team, the people who are waiting their turns should be:

- paying attention to the speaker;
- reacting to what the other person is saying;
- sensitive to an error;
- ready to stand in;
- able to correct a technical problem.

Too often the speakers who have gone first are so relieved to have survived the ordeal that they sit down, blow out a deep breath, let their shoulders sag and look totally uninterested in what their colleagues are saying. Sometimes they even talk to team members seated next to them.

For the audience to be interested in the talk, you should be interested in it, too. Think about paintings you have seen in which there is a central figure with several others positioned around him or her. All eyes are directed toward that figure. The artist is directing you, the viewer, by having attention focused on the main person.

In the same way, consider yourself part of the piece of artwork. When you are not speaking, your attention should be on the speaker. You should nod in agreement or smile when a joke is told. Remember you are a team – not a group of individuals. Your visual commitment to your colleagues pays off. When audiences see that you are paying attention to the speech, they will too.

Nineteen
Visual Aids

Your visual aids may include a computer-generated presentation, slides, product samples, handouts, or videos. No matter what type of visual aid you choose, you should consider what you need and why you need to include it in your talk.

WAY 85   DECIDE WHAT YOU NEED

Some speakers believe that visuals are an essential part of every presentation. That isn't necessarily true. Such people make the assumption because they see other speakers use them all the time. You don't always need to include visuals in your talk. They can interfere.

Before deciding on whether or not to use visuals, think about the nature of your talk. Think about the message or messages that you want to get across. Think about the complexity of your ideas. Are you discussing a subject that is abstract or one that includes many calculations? These are two instances when having visuals might clarify your point or might reinforce your ideas. Go through your talk and decide what aspects would benefit from some sort of visual reinforcement. Think about all your options and then determine what type of aid will help you in getting your message across:

- Should everyone have a copy of the budget?
- Would a pie chart make your ideas clearer?
- Would three key points on a slide or transparency emphasize your main points?
- Would a photograph help?
- Would a column of numbers on a flip-chart clarify your analysis?

- Would a product sample or model make a difference?
- Would a bar graph or a figure from a report explain your point?
- Should you show a video to reinforce your message?

If your message is simple, don't use any visuals. There may be no need.

WAY 86   KEEP YOUR AUDIENCE IN MIND

If you decide to use visuals, never forget your audience. Visuals are designed for the audience, not for you. If you do decide to use visuals:

- Consider the nature of the room and the size and composition of the group. You want to be sure that everyone in every seat can see every letter or picture that you show them.
- You want everyone to see what you have written without their squinting. Keep your images simple.
- Keep your bullet points consistent. If you begin the first one with a verb, then have the others start with a verb. If your bullets begin with nouns, then all of them should begin with nouns.
- The audience will have trouble deciphering slides and transparencies that are overloaded with numbers or graphs.
- Transparencies and slides with multiple paragraphs or with 10 or 12 sentences on them are hard to read.
- Actual pages of reports projected on a screen are hard to read.
- Visuals that are all capital letters are difficult to decipher.
- If the visuals confuse, then they are not serving your purpose.

Sometimes speakers use their visuals as if they were cue cards for themselves in place of using note cards. Such visuals are designed for the presenter, not for the audience.

In addition, be sure that your choice of visual is appropriate for the group. Sometimes cartoons or photographs appeal to a certain segment of the population but not to the whole group. Like with so much of presentation, make careful decisions.

WAY 87   GUIDE YOUR AUDIENCE

If you project a visual on a screen, the audience may look at any part of the projected image. Help them. Guide them by telling them where to look. 'If you look at the lower half of the screen…', 'Please look at the segment on the pie chart which represents 25 per cent', 'If I can direct you to the second paragraph…'. Each of these phrases helps the audience to stay with you. Of course, you can point, but laser pointers are not popular with everyone for many reasons, the least of which is that they can be distracting. Your finger or a pointer may be offensive or may shake. So your words are often the best way to direct your listeners.

Beware of falling into the trap of turning to point out something on the screen. You will discover that your back is completely turned to the audience. Your voice is projected back toward the screen rather than forward into the room. You have also clearly lost eye-contact.

Handouts are wonderful if you want people to have the opportunity to recall what you have said when you and they are no longer together. They are also an excellent place for your audience to write notes, so leave enough white space on them.

However, if you don't control when and how you are going to use them, they can be a nuisance. When you distribute them is important. If you leave handouts on chairs or on table tops before you talk, people will begin to read them. In fact, you may find that they are reading them as you are talking. Thus, sometimes it is better to wait until you have begun your talk to distribute them and then to guide the audience through their use as you would your other images. When you time your run-through, don't forget to include referring to samples or handouts. They add time.

WAY 88   DOUBLE CHECK YOUR WORK

Nothing can kill a good presentation faster than an error on a visual. People enjoy finding spelling or grammatical errors. The trouble is that they begin to look for more errors or question the accuracy of your other figures. Be sure that what you have prepared is accurate and correct. Be sure that the spelling is 'despair' and not 'dispair'. Be sure that you meant 'it's' and not 'its'. Check that you meant 'their' instead of 'there'. Check the spelling of names. Be sure that you have the correct dates.

In addition to the correct spelling and dates, put titles on your graphs and charts. Again, don't assume that your audience will be concentrating all the time or that everyone will be present from the start of your talk. If you put a title on a chart, you help the audience to follow you and to remember.

Twenty
Intangibles

It is all well and good to talk about specific issues like your use of 'ems', your putting your hand in your pocket or selecting the type size for your visuals. However, there are other aspects to making a presentation that are not as easily quantified or analysed. Let's call them the 'intangibles'. Let's consider three: honesty, warmth and caring.

WAY 89   BE HONEST

Tell the truth. Now that really must sound like an outrageous statement. We are not talking about avoiding deliberately misrepresenting your product's safety or your range of services; not at all. In this instance, 'being honest' means being careful not to stretch the truth. It is easy to do. Sometimes in your desire to give a good presentation you make remarks that are not 100 per cent true, accurate or validated.

It can happen if you have had to prepare your presentation to a tight deadline. Despite your best efforts, you may not have had all the data that you need to support your arguments. Thus, what you have may be incomplete. If that is the case, rather than letting the audience make assumptions, tell them at the outset what your limitations or your parameters are. Say 'I will not be discussing…' or, 'I will only be focusing on… not on…'. Don't present your material as if it were a complete and thorough analysis if it isn't.

'Why is this necessary', you ask. Because you don't want to be caught in a lie or in a minor misrepresentation. If you say that 'Everyone agreed that…' when you don't have enough data to know if they did or didn't agree, then you shouldn't. The audience will doubt the rest of your ideas. As you know, once one aspect of your work is suspect, then the accuracy of your findings and ultimately the wisdom of your recommendations are called into question.

What is at stake is your credibility. You do not want to damage your own reputation or that of your organization. The value of your good name can not be measured. Reputation and credibility are difficult to repair once they've been damaged. Protect yourself and your organization by providing accurate information.

WAY 90 BE WARM

We have all experienced times when we are put off by other people's behaviour. Ever enter a country, walk through immigration or customs and find yourself wondering what crime you have committed or are suspected of carrying out? Have you entered a country and been greeted by a smiling, pleasant officer who welcomes you? Amazing how that smile makes a difference. In the first situation you may feel demeaned; in the second, you feel good. The same is true for presentations:

- Speakers who appear cold seem to be indifferent.
- Speakers who never smile appear stiff.
- Speakers who never look at their audiences may appear bored.
- Speakers who never make eye-contact or who look out the window or at the back wall may appear to be aloof.

You motivate the audience to be interested in you and your words. You do this by your demeanour. Audiences want you to look as if you are enjoying the moment and are glad to be with them. That doesn't mean that you should laugh if you are conveying bad news about a plant closure or a salary freeze.

Of course, you should feel for the people with whom you are speaking. Convey empathy or sympathy not only in your words but in your smile. Laugh if the occasion warrants it. Gesture. Nod your head. As we said before, if you make an error, laugh at yourself. Make the correction and take it in your stride. In sum, show with simple facial expressions or by your demeanour that you are a human being, not some sort of automaton.

WAY 91   CARE

Demonstrate to the audience that you care about them and your topic. The best way to do this is to take time in preparing your presentation and paying attention to detail. Give a professional presentation. Show them that their opinion of you matters, too.

- Check your work for errors of any kind.
- Be sure that you have the correct spelling and pronunciation of names.
- Handle your material with pride.

Some speakers start by unfolding crumpled notes. Others toss their notes on the table as they finish. Still others leave their materials strewn around after a talk, as if those slides or samples were of no consequence to anyone. These gestures suggest a cavalier attitude. Those materials should matter to you. They matter to the audience. Those papers represent hours of work. You should not let them believe that you feel your paperwork or your audience are of no consequence.

Be aware of what is happening around you and respond. Be attentive to every question you are asked. Don't be indifferent to the questioner. Listen intently and respond with enthusiasm to the questioner and to the audience. You will be viewed as a concerned and committed professional.

Twenty-one
The Big Day

Eventually the day on which you are scheduled to speak will arrive. It is inevitable. Up until now you have been assembling and organizing your material. You have also spent time practising the actual delivery. Now it's different. You are facing the actual moment. This time your run-through isn't for timing or emphasis. It's the real thing. It's show time.

WAY 92   CHECK THE ROOM

Hopefully you have already checked the room for the acoustics and the layout. On the day, however, you would do well to get into the room early to check it once more. You do not want to discover when you are starting your talk that there is no paper on the flip-chart, that you have no markers, or that someone took the table you requested and has replaced it with a lectern. When you carry out your check, be sure that:

- You are not going to trip over any flexes that are lying in your path.
- The chairs are organized the way you thought they would be.
- No loud event is scheduled for the room next door, like a party, construction work, or a show.
- The room is light or dark enough for you to use your equipment or read your notes.
- Your equipment is working.
- Your glass of water is accessible but not so near that you could knock it over the equipment or it could fall off the edge of the table.

- Check the sight lines again to be sure that everyone can see you and your visuals.
- If you are using a lectern, be sure that it isn't too tall for you. You don't want the audience to see only a talking head.
- Test the microphones. Test them again.

If a meal will be served while you are speaking, be prepared to pause while dishes are served or removed. Look at the thermostat to be sure that the room is neither too hot nor too cold. Open a window if the room is too hot or stuffy. If you can't adjust the temperature, you may have to adapt your presentation because of the audience's discomfort.

You get the idea. Survey the area. The more often you give presentations, the speedier the survey. The details won't be the same for every talk, and every room has its own idiosyncrasies. However, you will discover that a brief survey will eliminate surprises. You have enough to worry about without aggressive flexes lying in wait.

WAY 93   AGREE ON THE PROTOCOL

Once again, the devil is in the details. Find out if you are introducing yourself or being introduced by someone else. Sometimes you may prefer to incorporate your own introduction into your opening remarks. On other occasions, you may prefer to have someone else introduce you. In the first instance, you may want to explain why your experience qualifies you to speak on the subject.

If you are being introduced by someone else, don't assume anything. Be sure that the introduction is the one that you want. Sometimes the person who is making the introduction is inaccurate about your background or about your presentation. Be sure that their remarks are both true and correct. MCs have been known to indicate that the speaker is going to talk about one subject when the topic is not what the speaker intended talking about at all. The audience ends up bewildered and disappointed.

Sometimes you don't want the MC to give away too much. 'Today John will be showing us a video of the new...'. Well, maybe you wanted the video to be a surprise. That's why it's important you compare notes with the MC beforehand.

Be sure that you know the name and the correct pronunciation of the person who is introducing you. It is polite and gracious for you to say the person's name, rather than just saying, 'Thank you for the introduction.'

Be sure that there are no changes in the seating arrangements. You may have planned to be seated at the front, but the organizer has you on a dais. In addition, ask the organizer if you are going to be selecting questioners or if someone else will be recognizing people for you. What you don't want is to look unprepared or foolish when all eyes are on you.

WAY 94   HANDLE MISTAKES

Mishaps occur. You skip a line. You mispronounce a word. You forget to move to the next slide. A bulb burns out. There is a squeal over the microphone. Your stomach grumbles. You sneeze. Whatever it is, it's not the end of the world. However, if you try to over-compensate or hide the slip or faux pas from the audience, it may become a problem. Rather than sympathizing with you, the audience becomes uncomfortable for you.

Do what you normally do in the situation. If you sneeze or cough, excuse yourself. If you need a drink of water, have one. If you lose your place, excuse yourself and find it. More than likely the audience will be charmed by the fact that you are human too.

Don't interpret this recommendation to mean that you should deliberately make a mistake, or not worry about the audience's perception of you if you make lots of errors. While the audience may be charmed by your losing your place or train of thought once, they may become resentful or impatient if you do so three or four times. Naturally, they will begin to wonder if you value them and how much time you spent preparing your presentation.

WAY 95   REACT

Yes, you have a plan. And we all know about 'the best laid plans'. They can and do go awry. You can not plan for everything. You will have to react spontaneously to the situation you are in. Remember that one of the reasons you are making eye-contact is so that you can see what is happening in front of you. You will have to change your plan in some way if:

- the audience is getting tired;
- they look bewildered;
- they appear not to hear;
- they didn't get your joke;
- they are turning to each other for clarification;
- all eyes are focused somewhere other than you.

If all eyes are focused elsewhere, you have to stop. You have to look where the audience is looking to find out what is happening. Then deal with it.

Suppose everyone is staring at a door to your right. You can't keep on talking. You have to look at the door and see what is going on. Perhaps you have to open it. Maybe someone is trying to get in. There could be someone signalling to a friend in the room. Handle whatever happens.

If you see people leaning forward with their heads cocked as if to hear you better, you may have to speak louder. If people look bored, you may have to speed up, slow down, stop – do something. If people look confused you may have to repeat what you said or offer some clarification.

In other words, the audience's behaviour on the day may tell you that you have to make some kind of change to ensure that they pay attention to your message. It's all well and good just wanting to get through your presentation, but remember your objective is to be sure that the audience hears and comprehends your message. You do not want them to simply endure the experience like an unpleasant trip to the headteacher's office.

WAY 96   ENJOY YOURSELF

Once you are over the jitters that you will be experiencing in the first few minutes, enjoy what you are doing. Think about it. Speaking to a group means you have an opportunity to make a difference to other people's lives. Smile, look around and react to what is going on.

- If you suddenly recall a joke while you're speaking, you might work it in, even if you hadn't planned to use it.
- If you can remember an anecdote that might serve as a case study to clarify your point and it doesn't take too long to tell, tell it.
- When you speak, remember to smile, to move around, to use your arms and hands. Be animated.
- If something unusual happens while you are speaking – the lights go out, a phone rings, a bird flies in the window, someone makes a telling or amusing comment – don't be brittle. Enjoy the moment. Laugh if it's appropriate.

Of course, if your presentation is on a painful subject, you'd be hard pressed to enjoy yourself. But view the situation as an opportunity to make a change. Most presentations are not onerous. They are usually opportunities for you to motivate your listeners. Your joy, human-ness and enthusiasm will be contagious.

Twenty-two
When it's Over

Believe it or not, there will come a time when the talk is over. The questions have stopped. You have been thanked and have returned to your seat. Your presentation is over. But for a good speaker, it shouldn't be over.

WAY 97   BE PROUD

Be pleased with what you've done. Your talk may not have been perfect. You may have made a mistake. You may not have handled a question as well as you wanted to do. Nevertheless, be pleased. We are all excellent at finding fault with what we do. So, please don't resume your seat, wipe your brow, look at your feet and shake your head in disgust. Don't let a soul know that you are in any way disappointed with your performance. You don't want the audience to feel sympathy for you. You want them to think about what you told them.

You should look pleased. The truth is that you should be. Why? You have worked hard. You have done your homework. You have prepared. You have practised. You have survived a highly stressful experience. Be proud of yourself for doing that. Accept the fact that every time you present you will want to change some aspect of what you did. Speaking is an evolutionary process.

WAY 98   RE-EVALUATE

To improve you need to learn from what you did. Certainly, you can berate yourself. You can applaud yourself. But to develop, you should not just accept the applause from the audience, or settle for the thanks from your host and say to yourself 'It's over.' For a good speaker, when the speech is over, the thinking isn't over. When a few hours or a few days have gone by, think about your talk. Assess what you might have handled differently You can determine some of that by reflecting on the audience's reaction during your speech. You can also think about some of the questions that you were asked.

During the questioning, did the audience focus on a specific aspect of your presentation? Ask yourself if one of your points needed more clarification. In retrospect perhaps you spent too much time on topics that they understood and not enough on others. Think back:

- Did everyone laugh at your jokes or appear to relate to your stories? Did you tell too many? Were they all appropriate?
- Did you find yourself going off at a tangent? Ask yourself how that happened.
- Do you think that all the visuals were effective? Ask yourself which ones worked and which ones didn't. Were they clear?
- Did the talk flow naturally, or in retrospect, would you have eliminated some points and added others?

In light of what happened, would you decline an invitation for such a time or in such circumstances, if you were asked again?

WAY 99   GET FEEDBACK

In addition to doing your own reflecting on the event, ask colleagues whom you trust what they thought. Ask members of the audience. When they tell you that you were 'super' or 'grand', be wary. Don't settle for that. Being told that they 'thoroughly enjoyed it' or that you were 'marvellous' doesn't teach you anything. Sure, those comments may make you feel good, but what you want are specifics to learn from.

You will have to probe and ask 'Why?' and 'How?' You want information that will help you modify what you do for the next presentation. In addition, evaluate the outcome. Did you get the new client? Did your staff do what you want? Did the board consider your recommendations? In other words, was your message taken seriously and acted upon, or were you ignored?

WAY 100   WATCH AND LISTEN

Besides reflecting on what you did and asking your colleagues what did or didn't work for them, you should also get in the habit of watching other speakers. There are any number of opportunities to do just that:

- You can watch them on television.
- You can look at them at the cinema.
- You can attend talks, sermons, seminars and lectures.

Watch and learn from what you are seeing and hearing. Study other people's techniques:

- Watch how someone moves and how the audience reacts to that movement.
- Notice how speakers use or don't use their voices.
- Notice the speaker's choice of clothing.
- Look for the speaker's idiosyncrasies.
- Evaluate the creative use of visuals, handouts, samples or models.
- See what the speaker does to keep the audience's attention.

But most important, watch the audience. Pay attention to how the audience responds. Look around. Notice if side conversations are taking place. Notice if the audience is attentive, falling asleep or daydreaming. Notice if they are taking notes or doodling. Ask yourself why whatever is happening is happening. Then consider what the speaker might do or might have done to change the outcome. Consider trying it in the future.

Bear in mind, however, we are all individuals and what works for you as a speaker may not work for someone else, and vice versa. You may not be able to burst balloons or smoke a pipe without feeling foolish. Don't try a technique just because someone else did. Instead reflect on what you see and incorporate modifications of those ideas into your own repertoire. Select only those techniques with which you are comfortable.

- Perhaps you don't stop or pause enough.
- Perhaps you could vary your speed.
- Perhaps you should stop talking more often when you use visual images.
- Perhaps you will try a mnemonic or have the audience engage in an activity at the beginning.

WAY 101   DO IT AGAIN

And again and again. Look for opportunities to talk. The more often you speak, the more adept you will become. Remember that learning to be an excellent speaker is like learning any other new skill. Don't try to master it all at once. Work on one aspect of presenting at a time. For example, first you may want to focus on your voice or on improving your posture. When you feel that you have made some changes, then work on another aspect. Perhaps you think that you could use your hands more effectively. Maybe you want to organize your thoughts differently. Work on that next.

In other words, identify each of your strengths as a speaker. Be conscious of them and use them. Then, identify weaknesses and eliminate them one at a time. The nervousness won't go. The dread will. Your confidence will grow, too, as you have more and more of these experiences behind you. You will recognize that you can give a good presentation. Certainly you will know that the floor will not open up and swallow you. You know that you can survive. You also know that you can make a difference to your audience.

Find opportunities to talk. Even if it is only for five minutes, or even 10, speak. The more you do, the better you will become. The more frequently you plan, speak and reflect on your audience's reaction the better. It is for your development. The more often you speak, the more effective you will become as a speaker.

Index

Visit Kogan Page on-line

Comprehensive information on
Kogan Page titles

Features include

- complete catalogue listings,
  including book reviews and
  descriptions

- special monthly promotions

- information on NEW titles and
  BESTSELLING titles

- a secure shopping basket facility
  for on-line ordering

PLUS everything you need to know
about KOGAN PAGE

http://www.kogan-page.co.uk